Scientific and Medical Studies
on the
Apparitions at Medjugorje

D1439806

René Laurentin & Henri Joyeux

Scientific and Medical Studies
on the
Apparitions at Medjugorje

VERITAS

English language edition
first published 1987 by
Veritas Publications
7-8 Lower Abbey Street
Dublin 1

Original French language edition
published 1985 by
Editions OEIL
Paris

ISBN 0 86217 213 6

Translation: Luke Griffin
Typesetting: Printset & Design Ltd
Printed in the Republic of Ireland by
Mount Salus Press Ltd, Dublin

Contents

Preface

Ecstasies have never been subjected organically to scientific tests. This book is a 'first' in the field. It offers precise confirmation that the ecstasy of the young people of Medjugorje is neither dream nor epilepsy, hallucination nor hysteria, nor catalepsy. There is nothing pathological about it; they suffer no identity crisis.

This study is the fruit of ongoing dialogue between the medical team of Professor Henri Joyeux and the theologian editor of this book. The reader will readily distinguish the part played by each side: the syntheses are the work of the theologian while the tests and detailed reports are the responsibility of the medical team. The 'I' or 'we' will underline certain finer precisions which are not differences but which may help to indicate the role or perspective of each side.

We make no attempt to compete with the work of the Commission appointed by the Bishop of Mostar. Our sole aim is to cooperate; science is international and the Church catholic — indeed ecumenical. We freely admit to a certain fear in undertaking our task, mindful that the ending of the apparitions would remove all future opportunities for ever.

Our Croatian friends will pardon us for having acted as trans-frontier doctors and theologians; our sole preoccupation has been to serve their Church and their country which we hold more precious than any modest contribution we might make. We in no way wish that our studies should anticipate the judgment of the authorities. Our studies are sectoral while the final judgment on the events will be all-embracing. What helped to motivate our work is the fact that in the final analysis, according to the well-defined statutes of tradition and councils, the Bishop's decision does not carry the full dogmatic authority of his magisterium but rather depends on good judgement and the weight of the arguments.

This book is meant to be accessible to non-specialists. Legal statements and technical details are confined to an appendix. It is our hope that the facts ascertained and verified will clarify the meaning of this event which has moved and converted so many people from so many different nations in a fashion completely out of proportion to the unusual adventure of five

1

young people from a village hidden in a country that is officially marxist.

For this reason Monsignor Laurentin and other Bishops who have recognised the validity of apparitions have proposed their conclusions not as a dogma — as it were under pain of anathema — but rather as a reasoned judgment offered to Christians to be shared, improved, refined, even contested, if their arguments were to prove lacking in exactitude.

We therefore dedicate this scientific work dealing with a spiritual fact and of concern to the conscience of Christians world-wide, to the Church authorities whom we do not wish to bypass.

— To Monsignor Zanic of Mostar, responsible before God for the final judgement, as the successor of the Apostles in this place where the apparitions have produced incontestable fruits;

— To Cardinal Kuharic, Archbishop of Zageb and to the Yugoslav Espiscopal Conference who prudently watch over these events at a national level.

— To his Holiness, Pope John Paul II, who oversees that charity so necessary for discernment and who has graciously accepted our earlier works.

This study remains open to all the critical, scientific and theological contributions which are desirable in these matters.

Introduction

Why this book?

Why undertake scientific and, particularly, medical studies of the apparitions at Medjugorje? Is it not incongruous to submit phenomena that are sacred — or presumed to be — to laboratory experiments? This objection weighed heavily on us and indeed on the visionaries who were loath to become guinea pigs in an experiment.

And yet the task needed to be undertaken.

A doctor friend of mine experienced enormous difficulty in treating members of his immediate family. When someone fell ill in his household it was understood that the neighbouring doctor would be called. One day the latter was not available and my doctor friend went against the grain and treated a member of the family as a matter of emergency.

Testing the apparitions at Medjugorje seemed to us both urgent and necessary:

— *Urgent*, because, firstly, the commission appointed by the Bishop had not (at the time of writing) become active and, secondly, it would be impossible to carry out tests on the ecstasies once the apparitions had ended.

— *Necessary*, because the state of ecstasy poses many questions which, in many respects, can only be answered by medical science.

Only medical science can describe accurately the significantly physical phenomenona of ecstasy.

— It verifies its coherence (or its non-coherence);

— It verifies its normal or pathological character and the conditions required for it.

— Finally, even if the ecstasy is — as the visionaries feel it to be — a sacred phenomenon that transcends ordinary communications and perceptions — medicine and psychiatry ought not to give up; these phenomena still take place in the physical and psychic lives of the visionaries. They present themselves for clincal observation; thus medical science is fully within its rights to observe them. It is of the essence of scienfitic inquiry not to reject any fact no matter how paradoxical it may appear. If it turns out that the visionaries are right and, with the help of grace, perceive a person who is invisible to ordinary observers, then normal scientific observation will not reach this object but at least boundaries will have been set to the possible usefulness of scientific instruments. In other words, science can reach the receiver (visionaries) but it cannot read the transmitter who is perceived by the receiver alone. Thus, by identifying the conditions surrounding the visionaries' perceptions, the phenomenon will be more clearly defined and many possible hypotheses eliminated. Hallucination in the medical (pathological) sense is one such hypothesis.

These were our reasons for undertaking the studies, despite our reluctance to mix scientific experiment with a sacred phenomenon defined in terms of prayerful encounter.

As we were undertaking our studies we were further motivated by an external factor. Civil and ecclesiastical influences in Yugoslavia conspired to throw suspicion on publications favourable to Medjugorje and a theologian reviewing my first book took me to task for not being sufficiently scientific.[1] In fact this earlier work had no great scientific pretensions; it was based on earlier intuitions and was intended purely as a preparatory evaluation. The present studies were already under way when Professor Curic was reviewing my work. His article gave our work a further stimulus. It is hoped that this work will meet his criticisms. It is also to be hoped that Professor Curic will be able to prove that his criticism was not merely ritual rejection but was, rather, aimed at promoting truth alone.

Our contribution will be lost forever if the apparitions cease before the episcopal commission has undertaken a scientific study. Without such a study the phenomenon will remain an enigma forever, open to all kinds of objections and hypotheses. On the other hand, our tests close off many false avenues of investigation for any future investigator of this mysterious phenomonon.

Medical science plays a central role here. Most credit is due to Professor Henri Joyeux, hospital surgeon and director of a nutrition and experimental cancer laboratory. He conceived the medical approach, in dialogue with the theologian, who continually raises a series of questions. In conjunction with his colleagues and collaborators he set up and executed the tests, the

---

1. Josif Curic, Professor at the Jesuit Institute of Philosophy at Zagreb, 'Scientific Research at Medjugorje?' in *Obnovljeni Zivot (Renewed Life)*, a bimonthly on religious life, 29 (1984) No. 3-4. The author makes methodological remarks on the relationship between science and faith and tends to draw clear lines of distinction. In theory and in practice, while respecting the distinctions which he makes, I am more inclined to distinguish in order to unify. While scientific method has to be rigorous and without interference, the light of faith, while not providing any new elements for observation, may help to clarify the questions to be asked, the texts to be chosen and the meaning to be understood.

results of which are given in this book. This is how he defines the objective of this research:

> Ecstasy is seen as a sensory perception of realities that are perceivable by and visible to the visionaries but invisible to and imperceivable by all others and, in particular, those who seek to understand. For the first time in history science can study these facts as they unfold in Medjugorje and not merely *a posteriori*. The most advanced medical techniques and the most up-to-date photographic and cinematographic techniques help us to reach the kernel of these events in order to try to understand them.

Medical science provides the instruments which best isolate the bodily (and, therefore, measurable) aspects of the ecstasies at Medjugorje. Our book aims to broaden the horizon somewhat, in order to include further questions raised by the apparition which, to varying degrees, belong to medical science.

We will therefore examine the phenomena of ecstasy, fasting, cures and luminosity, all of which are present at Medjugorje.

1. The phenomenon of *ecstasy* which yields information on the conditions of communication to the visionaries and their receptivity.

2. The practice of *fasting* which has been extended greatly during the past two years following on the invitation 'on the part of Our Lady'. We will examine both the physical and spiritual aspects of fasting, counter-indications, risks and benefits.

3. With regard to the *cures* at Medjugorje we simply try to pull together the strands of abandoned material. In the present state of confusion it seems necessary in the first instance to distinguish between those who see a miracle at every turn and those who systematically deny any miracle.

4. We will try to mark out the area of *luminous phenomena* experienced at Medjugorje. It is as difficult to explain them as it is to ignore them.

5. We had thought of taking up again, on the basis of historical and textual criticism, the problem of the oracles of Hercegovina, and of the two priests punished by the Bishop of Mostar. These problems have shrouded the real debate all too frequently. However, the wounds are still open so it may be as well to postpone this study. When the inaccuracies and misrepresentations are left behind, the message that comes through and is expressed more or less clearly is an invitation to reconciliation through prayer and charity. Everything else comes from human agitation or from the Evil One.

1

Ecstasy

The word 'ecstasy' describes a state of disconnection from the surrounding environment which, as far as the subject is concerned, conditions perceptions of another order: God and the divine world. The visionaries claim to see the Virgin, sometimes accompanied by Christ, in the light of God. For them, as for Bernadette at Lourdes, the light comes before the vision.

1. Description

Before defining the word 'ecstasy' it might be helpful to define its characteristics. These are surprising both for those who witness the ecstasy and for the visionaries themselves; of particular interest is the disconnection (incomplete) with the exterior world which seems to justify the word 'ecstasy', from the Greek *ex-stasis,* meaning 'to be on the outside'. Should we say outside oneself or outside the ordinary world? Is this to facilitate the perception of another world? Clinical observation will help to provide the answers to these questions.

Before the apparition
Meanwhile, every day, a little before 6.00 p.m. in the winter and before 7.00 p.m. in the summer, the visionaries come to the little chapel of the apparitions.

Before the apparition they enter the chapel, relaxed and aware of others. The video cassette which I edited for ENES Editions demonstrates this.

In the first filmed apparition (before April 1984) the visionaries, on entering, notice a little invalid who is uncomfortable in a standing position. Marija, one of the five, takes her gently by the arm and puts her in a better place. Then she makes a sign. The others ask for a chair from one of the rare people lucky enough to have a seat in the crowded chapel. Vicka and Jakov bring the chair quickly. Only when the little invalid girl is comfortably seated do they begin the prayers that mark the beginning of the apparitions.

In the second ecstasy recorded in the same cassette a poor sick woman, wrapped up in her own sufferings, enters ahead of the visionaries. The poor woman, lamenting her suffering, takes the place normally occupied by the visionaries. They exchange questioning looks for a moment. What can be done for this poor woman who is obviously suffering? They are not going to overpower her with good intentions. Very quickly they discover that she is completely absorbed in her own suffering and she does not really expect anything from them. They leave her there despite the noise of her crying which interrupts the silence and fervour of the place. Without further ado they begin their prayers. For them the apparition is not an obsession; it does not paralyse them but, on the contrary, continuously enlivens their charity.

To prepare themselves for the apparition the visionaries, standing, recite several Our Fathers, Hail Marys and Glory Bes until 'The Gospa' appears. During the early months they usually recited each prayer twice or three times before the apparition took place. Since the end of 1983, ecstasy begins before they have finished the first Our Father.

First phase: Contemplation or conversation
Suddenly their gaze, already fixed on the location of the apparition, becomes more intense. There are hardly any movements of the eyelids (other tests will be more precise on this disputed point). Their faces become almost imperceptibly brighter and turn towards the invisible speaker. They kneel down very naturally, all at the same moment. The movement is not perfectly synchronised, a fact that might be attributed to their differing reaction times, or the difference in their reflexes. But we have never noticed a signal being given.

Thus they enter into a first phase of the ecstasy. Some, in particular Ivan and Marija, simply contemplate; others, particularly Vicka and Ivanka, converse, sometimes together, with the apparition. Their lips can be seen moving but no voices are heard, just as it was with Bernadette at Lourdes. They were not conscious of this and were surprised when we questioned them about this unusual phenomenon. They believe they are speaking normally.

We are still looking for a Croatian deaf-mute in order to try to discover if we are dealing with a coherent language: this would appear to be certain in the case of Vicka. Monsignor Zanic often mimics her strongly accented speech, making this almost an objection in itself.

Second phase: Prayer with the apparition
Suddenly, all their voices become audible, and they say, in Croatian, 'who art in heaven'; 'hallowed be Thy name' etc.

The opening words, 'Our Father', are not pronounced. 'The Virgin says these words', the visionaries respond, when we question them. After the Our Father they recite the Glory Be 'with the Virgin', they say.

Third phase: Contemplation or conversation
Their voices disappear again for a second period of contemplation or conversation.

End of apparition
And suddenly the five pairs of eyes and the heads are raised (this is most noticeable in the case of Jakov, the smallest visionary). This detail would indicate that the Virgin appears to be very close, less than a metre away horizontally ($\pm$ 50 centimetres depending on the crowd which sometimes forces them to stand very near the altar).

2. Are we dealing with ecstasy?
Dr Stopar objects to the use of the word *'ecstasy'* in describing the phenomena on the grounds that, etymologically, ecstasy means to be 'outside oneself', 'outside the ordinary tangible world'.

The visionaries are evidently not outside themselves; they remain simple and natural. Their identity (consciousness), far from being altered, is merely intensified. It is an extremely lucid moment in their lives which is firmly retained in their memories. They maintain their equilibrium and their normal reactions in certain circumstances: if pushed they regain composure in the normal way. During the ecstasy itself they are able to pass on messages to the Virgin and, likewise, transmit her response to the petitioners.

Thus, they are not outside themselves in any sense that would convey alienation or *total* disconnection with the tangible world.

However, there is disconnection in many respects. Visual perception of the exterior world disappears. On 1 July 1981 Vicka and her two companions were locked in a police van. They remember quite clearly that their dismal surroundings disappeared as soon as the apparition appeared at the normal time. All they saw then was the Virgin. In the same way, Vicka is unable to say if the apparition is in front of the wall, behind the wall or even in the wall: she no longer sees the wall of the chapel of the apparitions (*from conversations with Fr Bubalo*). We will see that the interposition of a person or a screen or even the closure of their own eyes,[1] does not prevent their perception of the apparition.

We will also see that it would be simplistic to draw the hasty conclusion that the phenomenon is therefore subjective or of a hallucinatory nature. Clinical observation and other tests exclude this conclusion.

For these reasons, the word 'ecstasy' seems to me to be justified, though with the distinctions introduced by Boutroux ('Le Mysticisme', *Bulletin de l'Institut de Psychologie* 1902, pp. 15, 17):

---

1. Test carried out by Father Custic, editor-in-chief of *Glas Koncila*, in July 1981, during an apparition which took place in the presbytery.

'Ecstasy' is that state in which all communication with the outside world is broken. The soul senses that it is in communication with an internal object which is perfect Being, infinite Being, God... Ecstasy is the meeting of the soul with its object. There are intermediaries between the soul and Him. The soul sees, touches, possesses Him; the soul is in Him and part of Him. Faith no longer believes without seeing. It is more than science can achieve for science only grasps being in concrete objects: it is a perfect union in which the soul experiences a fullness of existence through that mechanism of self-giving and self-renunciation, for He to whom the soul gives itself is Being and Life itself.

Boutroux's definition applies strictly to mystical union with God. It therefore requires the following clarifications:

1.   At Medjugorje (just as at Lourdes and at Pontmain), communication with the outside world is only partially interrupted. The break with exterior reality is seriously modified to suit different circumstances.

2.   We are not dealing with a purely spiritual communication with God but with a *tangible* communication: the visionaries both see and hear the Virgin.

3.   Nor are we dealing with internal communication or with an internal object. The visionaries see a real person with a three-dimensional body, whom they have touched on more than one occasion.

It might be tempting to speak not of *ex-stasis*, but of *in-stasis*: a kind of interior absorption, based on the fact that the voices are inaudible to the exterior world; thus speaking remains a more intimate phenomenon during conversations with the Virgin Mary. This, however, would merely confuse the more general aspects of ecstasy in an attempt to pursue clarity on a very specific issue. The inaudibility of the voices is in any case a passing phenomenon, given the fact that the voices become audible during the recitation of the Our Father with Our Lady during the apparition. Other exceptions to the phenomenon of inaudibility included the transmission of questions to the Virgin and of her response to the public at the beginning of the apparitions. The point is that the visionaries are not focused on themselves. Their attitude is that of one who looks ardently at an exterior object or, more precisely, at a loved one with whom they communicate through the senses and, sometimes, tangibly.

We feel therefore that in a broad sense it is justifiable to speak of ecstasy, though narrower definitions might not permit this terminology. For example, Pierre Janet's definition:

(Ecstasy is)... a state which is characterised, from the physical point of view, by almost complete immobility, a diminution of all the functions by which we relate to others, of circulation and of breathing patterns; from the emotional point of view, there exists a feeling of happiness, of unspeakable joy ...which is extremely characteristic of this state (P. Janet, 'Un Ecstatique', in *Bulletin de l'Institut de Psychologue* 1901 229-30).

Even if the feeling of happiness and contentment is verified in the case of the visionaries of Medjugorje, other elements which Janet specifically requires are not present. There is no immobility, or diminution of the senses by which they relate to others and, as we shall see, there are no significant changes in their circulation and breathing patterns. These differences may well be attributable to the fact that Pierre Janet based his observations almost entirely on the psychically disturbed and their subjective ecstasies.

As was the the case with Bernadette there are also moments of shared sadness when the apparition speaks of sin, or of the calamity that will befall the world. The joy which they experience is therefore not mindless euphoria nor is it superficial. It increases their receptivity and gives them strength in adversity.

Clinical observation has already shown that there is nothing pathological about this state. The visionaries enter into ecstasy without pain or stress. During the ecstasy they remain quite natural: they are not tense, nor anxious nor cataleptic. This strikes many observers. Their prayer is robust and without affectation. In a word, they are at their best.

Thousands of real life observations and video recordings indicate that no signals are given and there are no indications of play-acting. The apparition comes and goes without apparent reason. Its duration varies from fifty seconds to three quarters of an hour, although no apparition has lasted for more than one or two minutes since the end of 1983. The apparition appears without advance notice in the light which precedes it; it disappears likewise, so that no hard and fast rule can be deduced as to how long it will last, whether it will be fifty-four seconds or three quarters of an hour.

3. Benefits of the tests

Above and beyond simple clinical observation, what other benefits can be derived from medical tests which, to repeat what we have said, reach only the receivers and not the transmitter, she whom they see?

The tests allow us to verify the effects of this state on the brain, the heart, the circulation system, the eyes and the visual mechanisms, the hearing, the larynx,, vocal activity etc. They allow us to grasp the continuation of the natural, habitual state and, at one and the same time, the particular characteristics of this second state: in particular this relative disconnection from the exterior world which is a condition for the perception of an apparition, since only the ecstatics see this vision.

Apart from the six visionaries, one of whom, Mirjana, has not witnessed the apparition since 25 December 1982, only two other people, to my knowledge, have seen the apparition. One was Jozo Zovko, who saw the apparition several times in the chapel and later in prison. The second was a person who was passing through, whose unique apparition, being of a totally personal nature, must remain secret even though it has profoundly changed that person's life.

Before examining the tests which Professor Henri Joyeux, together with his colleagues and myself, has set up we ought to examine previous medical tests with a view to evaluating the phenomenon further and defining as far as possible its element of mystery.

4. First medical examinations
Examinations required by the police (27 & 29 June 1981)

The first examinations of the visionaries were required by the police of Citluk. This initiative was normal and should not be interpreted as undue interference by a marxist regime. In the face of such facts any administration can legitimately ask: is this normal or pathological? If one were in the presence of a psychosis, then the interests of public health would justify submitting the entire affair to a psychiatrist. Prefect Massy, who was a Catholic, had Bernadette undergo an examination by three doctors on 27 March 1958. He had even endeavoured to anticipate the outcome by indicating that the diagnosis should be one of alienation. He then invited the commission to issue a certificate that would enable him to have Bernadette committed to a psychiatric hospital. They did not comply but their embarrassment at trying to meet the dictates of the Prefect is evident in their report. At Medjugorje police procedures were far more normal.

On Saturday 27 June 1981, before the sixth apparition, Dr Ante Bijevic carried out the first medical examination at Citluk. He found the visionaries to be well balanced.

Vicka describes how she succeeded in hastening the end of the examination which had gone on for some time. Dr Bijevic was taking some time with his examination of Ivan. She entered, eager to see the end of the whole thing.

'Is it not finished?'
'It is not your turn, but you may sit down.'
'Thanks be to God, I am young and healthy, I can remain standing. And then, when I do need a medical examination, I'll come of my own accord. Now, is it all over?'

Her good sense convinced the doctor and he allowed her to go.

On 29 June the second and final examination took place. The visionaries were taken to a psychiatric hospital in Mostar. They were examined by a woman, Dr Dzuda. The examination seems to have taken place early in the morning. The young people were taken there just as they were

11

preparing for morning Mass at St Peter's. The examination lasted until two in the afternoon. According to Vicka Dr Dzuda concluded: 'It is the people who brought you here that are insane. You are absolutely normal.'

The reports of these two first examinations are, of course, not available.

A psychological study of Slavko Barbaric

In 1982 Slavko Barbaric, a doctor of social psychology, published a methodical analysis of the group of visionaries in *Zbornil Krsni Zavicaj*, no. 15, subsequently translated into Italian in *De Apparizioni di Medjugorje*, Milan, Mimep-docete 1984, pp88-105. This summary, which is summarised by Father Rupcic in the book which we wrote jointly, *La Vierge apparait-elle a Medjugorje?*, establishes two conclusions:

1.   The group of young people is disparate; there are boys and girls, of different ages and of extremely different temperaments. The phenomenon is not explicable as the action of a leader, nor as the activity of an external manipulator but only as the apparition which forms and directs the group. Ecstasy has not diminished but rather enhanced the identity and freedom of the visionaries and this includes their vocation. They understand the desire of the Virgin but she has left them free and they in turn feel absolutely free to make their own decisions.

2.   The apparitions show no signs of hallucination; neither the character nor the psychological profile of the young people, their history nor their lifestyle provide an argument in favour of hallucination. The tests exclude the hypothesis.

Dr Stopar's inquiry

Dr Stopar is a psychiatrist and parapsychologist. He studied general medicine at Gratz and psychiatry and hypnotherapy in Berlin. He undertook further studies in parapsychology in Fribourg and then became director of the Polyclinic of Maribor in Yugoslavia. He came to Medjugorje to examine the visionaries on four occasions. Each of his visits lasted from five to ten days, in May and November, 1982 and in June and November, 1983.

He wrote only a very brief report (which we reproduce in an appendix together with the text of two interviews which we had with Dr Stopar in the spring of 1984: p. 112). He confined himself to observation and to tests without equipment and of a non-quantifiable nature. The results of his examination, which was essentially parapsychological, can be summed up as follows:

The neuro-psychiatric, medico-psychological and somatological tests to which these young people were subjected showed them to be absolutely normal and there were no psycho-pathological indications.

One of the visionaries, Marija, was subjected to hypnosis and the test proved that there was no difference between her conscious account and her automatic account under hypnosis. This of course excludes both play-acting and manipulation.

These phenomena show objective characteristics and would indicate a transcendent origin (report of December 1982).

Thus, Dr Stopar comes to a limit which is an invitation to go beyond. He argues up to this limit as a 'theist parapsychologist'. These phenomena are less well explained by having recourse to unknown natural forces than by postulating a higher, divine order.

Dr Phillipe Madre's impression

Dr Madre was in Medjugorje from Tuesday 23 August to the evening of Thursday 25 August. He was well qualified to examine the facts. He is the founder of a special clinic in Castres where studies of theological discernment and of somatic factors are undertaken. He came more as a deacon than as a doctor. His aim was to introduce the parish of Medjugorje to the charism of healing. He was accompanied by two priests, Fr Emiliano Tardif and Fr Pierre Raucourt, both Canadians. They were, however, arrested by the police on the day after their arrival and were deported. Dr Madre was therefore unable to give anything more than a general impression based on intuition. He comes down unreservedly in favour of the visionaries' physical and psychic health and also notes their spiritual development, especially in the case of Marija.

Important developments were made by the Italian doctors who came in large numbers in 1984:

Dr Maria Frederica Magatti, 3-4 February and 22 March 1984

Dr Magatti witnessed the ecstasy on 3-4 February. She undertook a clinical analysis which she herself admitted was 'inadequate, and too quick'. The following is a summary of her findings: 'We are dealingwith ecstasy because during the events (the young people) lose contact with the surrounding world; they remained insensitive to stimulation: calling, touching, pinching — no response, not even an indication of pain in the case of pinching. A cine-projector of approximately 1000 watts was played on their eyes without causing any modification in the diameter of the pupils. Their eyelids continued to blink according to their natural rhythm (blinking occurred spontaneously if their faces were touched).

— From the point of view of movement:
Ivan's arm was raised; there was no resistance, but when it was released it returned to its former position by a voluntary movement.[1]

1. The test excludes catalepsy.

13

Jakov was lifted off the ground while he was kneeling. His legs straightened out, apparently hanging without muscular control. On being put back on the ground, the child spontaneously resumed the kneeling position (apparently by a voluntary movement).

— During the apparition there was no evidence of change in the vegetative nervous system. The heartbeat remained the same and there was neither perspiration nor tears. Any motor activity which remained was voluntary, in particular the movement of the lips during conversation with the apparition. 'From the foregoing we can deduce the absolute neurological normality of the visionaries in spite of the suspension of their consciousness of relationship with the exterior world' (in M. Botta, *Le Apparizione di Medjugorje*, Pessano, Milano, Mimep-docete, 1984 pp.85-6).

Dr Lucia Capello, 5-6 February, 23 March

Dr Capello, who lives in Mostar, was present at the apparitions on 5 and 6 February and on 23 March 1984. She observed Ivan, Jakov and Marija three times, Vicka twice and Ivanka once.

The following are her conclusions:

— there is no agitation, either psychic or of the motor function;

— there is no indication of psychic conditioning. The young people enter the room normally; they recognise and greet those who are present in a familiar, friendly fashion, almost indeed in an off-hand way (Marija, Ivan and especially Ivanka, depending on the temperament of each one). The same type of relationship continues after the apparition.

— Vicka, who was given closer attention by this doctor, remains detached from the outside world during the apparition, but her pulse is scarcely more rapid than before the ecstasy. In the same way her breathing remains normal. Her forehead is more or less cold. Vicka had no reaction to the examinations which were carried out.

— little Jakov did not offer the slightest resistance when he was raised 15 centimetres off the ground. He made no attempt to regain his balance either when he was lifted or when he was put down again. He returned to the kneeling position as if this were the point of maximum repose according to the laws of gravity. His attitude offered no evidence of preconditioning either in the recent or more distant past.

I did not meet with any type of frustration or, indeed, any ulterior motive on the part of the visionaries. They appeared to be discreet, well-mannered, careful in their dress and in their speech and absolutely mindful of the surroundings in which they found themselves. Their behaviour seemed to conform perfectly with that of young people of their own age (remarks published in *Le Apparizione di Medjugorje*, 1984 pp87-8).

In another article Dr Capello notes what she calls the 'three synchronisations' (the simultaneity of the key movements during ecstasy).

1. The visionaries drop to their knees, their voices become inaudible while their lips continue to articulate.

2. Their voices become audible at the same time, on the third word of the Our Father, the apparition having recited the first two. This phenomenon militates against the theory of a prior agreement and cannot be put down to natural causes.

3. The eyes and heads are raised at the end of the apparition with perfect simultaneity; the word *ode* ('she is going away'), which is pronounced by one or a number of visionaries, cannot be taken as a signal; sometimes it is not pronounced at all and sometimes it is pronounced simultaneously by a number of the children.

Conclusion: The first synchronisation could be explained (I say *could* but not *is*) by natural causes; the second and the third and, in particular, the second, have no natural explanation and indicate that there is something that is seen only by the visionaires and not by the observers.

Dr Mario Botta, 23-24 March 1984

1. Dr Botta, a heart surgeon from Milan, observed the visionaries on 8-9 December 1983 and took Ivan's pulse. In taking the pulse he pushed Ivan's watch strap up his arm and the boy seemed to be completely unaware of this. The pulse was normal.

2. On 23-24 March Dr Botta carried out an electrocardiogram on Ivan (a Holter test). The test began ten minutes before the apparition and continued until after the Mass which followed. At this point Ivan asked to have the equipment removed so that he could join his prayer group on the hill of Kriezevak. The prayer meeting had been arranged previously.

The frequency of the heart beat was from 74 to 110 pulsations per minute (P-Q 0,12).

Conclusion: Ecstasy does not suppress normal physiology but somehow transcends it, placing the visionary on a higher plane. It is therefore impossible to study apparitions using the ordinary method of diagnosing symptoms. The phenomenon calls for an openness of faith to the Virgin whom the visionaries claim to see (ibid. pp.108-110).

My meeting with Dr Botta

I was present at the test which took place on 23 March 1983. This was the first time I had met Dr Botta who had come with some Italian colleagues to administer a number of tests to the visionaries. We had lunch together, if one could call it lunch, for in the presbytery of Medjugorje the Friday fast permitted only bread and water. Incidentally, Dr Botta observes the same fast when at home in Milan. The conversation did not suffer. When, at the end of the ecstasy, the visionaries stood up, they said:

> 'The Virgin smiled at seeing him in harness. We asked her what she thought. She answered: "It is not necessary". Dr Botta was extremely attentive to the negative side of this statement.
>
> ' "Not necessary", does not mean that there is blame attaching', I said to him.
>
> Father Tomislav Vlasic agreed with this interpretation.
>
> The Virgin repeats ceaselessly that the essential is prayer. Everything else, including the tests, are accessories.

But Dr Botta was not convinced and he left, having completed only one test. The graph shows the perfect rhythm of the heartbeat during the apparition: 80-99 pulsations. Dr Botta tended to see in this a confirmation of his clinical tests according to which the apparitions of the Virgin 'transcend physiological reality, that is they leave it untouched'. There was an interruption in the curve after the apparitions but, as we later confirmed in our tests, this was entirely due to the mechanical fault in the equipment.

It was during this period (24-25 March) that I met Professor Henri Joyeux by appointment. It was then that we began to plan the further tests which would begin on 10 June.

Dr Enzo Gabrici, Neuro-psychiatrist, 4-8 April 1984

From 4-8 April Dr Gabrici examined Ivan, Jakov, Marija and Vicka (the latter was absent on the third day). He noted the sudden and simultaneous kneeling down, their gaze which is fixed on the cross and even slightly higher, and Vicka's conversation and gesticulation. Outside of the ecstasy he notes Vicka's handshake, her extremely normal style and the ease with which she responds. She says she does not see a vision or an image 'but a real person'; she 'hears a real voice' etc. The apparition has remained exactly the same since the beginning.

Vicka shows no signs of emotional hardship, human misunderstanding or previous traumas. The apparition does not tire her as is the case with hysterical trances; on the contrary, she feels more invigorated.

During a second apparition Vicka was absent. Dr Gabrici was particularly attentive to Jakov whose lips moved rapidly as if he were speaking.

There is not even a transitory alteration of their consciousness. Neither facial change, nor winking of the eyes nor any other sign could explain the synchronisation of their kneeling down. They all focus on the crucifix (placed rather high) and they kneel down together as if impelled.

The subjects are very normal in their ordinary lives (family, school and church). Little Jakov was somewhat tired after the long ceremony which followed the apparition and went out for a few moments to play with Dr Frigerio's children. Vicka is an equally normal subject with no traces of neurosis or psychosis. Clinical observation has also excluded hallucinatory phenomena as well as the normal components of epilepsy or of any other malfunction capable of producing the alteration of consciousness. There are no symptoms which would suggest that the subjects are living out something which was previously suggested under hypnosis. The visionaries can recall with absolute lucidity what has happened to them.

They are, as it were, rapt, at the moment of the apparition. They differ from mediums who are taken over by a different personality; the visionaries retain perfect consciousness of their identity. Their detachment from the surrounding environment is due to the fact that they are completely taken up by the apparition. Psychoanalysis brings no light to bear on this state of clarity of consciousness. In fact, the observations offer nothing which would foster doubt about the soundness of their perceptions.

Dr Anna Maria Franchini, 5 April 1984
Professor Franchini observed four of the visionaries — Ivan, Vicka, Marija and Jakov. The apparition took place a little before 7.00 p.m. (the scheduled time for the middle of spring to the beginning of autumn).

She notes:

— the convergence of their gaze on the cross;
— the smiles of Vicka and Jakov;
— the disappearance of the voices;
— the final raising of their eyes;

and concludes:
The group is made up of a number of independent individuals. Each has his or her own attitude but all are drawn towards an external object which holds their attention with an intensity which I have never up to this point experienced and which in my view characterises the uniqueness of the experience (ibid. pp.116).

5. The test carried out by Fr Nicholas Bulat (2 June)
In the meantime another test was undertaken by a member of the episcopal commission. Fr Bulat was not a doctor but a priest, Professor of Dogma at the Seminary of Split. The test which he undertook has nothing to do with modern medicine but has its origin in a tradition dating from the middle

ages. Observers had always been struck by the insensitivity of ecstatics to pain and came up with the idea of testing this insensitivity. They invented and reinvented three tests which always remained the same: burning, pinching, pricking. In Lourdes Bernadette had been pricked twice:

'On 23 February, Eleonore Peyrard stuck a long blackhead thorn in her shoulder without provoking the slightest reaction' (R. Laurentin, *Lourdes, Histoire authentique,* Vol. 4, p. 215).

'On another occasion, the date is uncertain, a futher witness, perhaps Dr Dozous, prodded her in the heel, according to the evidence of Julie Garros' (ibid Vol. 3, pp. 125-6, note 113).

At Medjugorje, in the absence of the medical commission which had never been convened in a formal meeting, it was Fr Bulat who conceived and executed, on his own initiative, the medieval test of prodding. On 2 June, wearing dark glasses, the priest entered the room of the apparitions a little before 6.00 p.m. Very few members of the commission had ever entered this room! He followed Vicka as she came in and took a seat right behind her. He carried a large needle in his left hand; this allowed him to make a quick sign of the cross with the visionaries as they began their prayers. He then switched the needle to his right hand, aimed it at Vicka's left shoulder blade and stuck it in. Under the sheer pressure of the action Vicka's body moved somewhat to the right but she quickly and gracefully regained balance. Not a muscle in her face moved. She continued her conversation with Our Lady, unperturbed. Fr Bulat has a second go. This time the pressure was perhaps a little less or was delivered from a better angle. To an observer placed in front the impact was less. Her face showed no reaction.

When we questioned Fr Bulat he said that he had noted some muscular movement in the neck, at least during the course of the second prod. But he was placed behind Vicka and too much on the vertical to be able to notice. It would appear that any movement was simply Vicka's effort to regain her balance after the pressure of the needle.

After the apparition, when Vicka got up to leave, a small blood stain, a little over a centimetre in diameter, was seen to mark the spot where the needle had penetrated. A video made by an amateur gives evidence of the stain.

The prod was deep. In that region of her body it would normally have provoked pain. Vicka should have cried out, observed Professor Joyeux when he saw the tape. As far as he is concerned, this ancient and brutal medieval test is of little significance. On the other hand, we do not regret that it has been carried out for, in a certain sense, it shows one of the properties of ecstasy in the visionaries of Medjugorje, just as was the case at Lourdes with Bernadette. It manifests a certain cultural continuity in these matters.

6. The tests carried out by Professor Henri Joyeux and his team from Montpellier

On the vigil of Pentocost, Saturday 9 June, Professor Henri Joyeux came to administer the first of his electro-encephalograms. I had arrived twenty-four hours earlier to prepare the ground but the police at Zagreb turned me back without any explanation. It was only later that I learned that the perpetrator, who has since lost his job, was acting out of fear in an incident far removed from the normal welcome offered to tourists in Yugoslavia. I was brought back to the Air France plane and put in first class for my involuntary return journey. Two hours later I found myself back in Paris. I was not, however, barred from this friendly country and so I made the journey again, this time by train and twenty-four hours of non-stop driving.

Suspense over permission from the visionaries

On arrival, three hours before the apparition, Dr Joyeux and I met with three of the visionaries — Jakov, Ivanka and Marija — to talk to them about our tests. We came up against a blank refusal by Jakov who spoke on behalf of the other two; the refusal was characterised by that solidarity so remarkable among the group:

> 'The Virgin said it was not necessary and Dr Botta did not continue his tests!'

We answered:

> 'It is not necessary for you or for those who believe but it is useful for those who do not believe and even for the Bishop who seems to think that we may be dealing with an hallucination or even a dream. The electro-encephalogram will eliminate these doubts one way or another. If you refuse this test then it would appear that you are afraid of the outcome. The Virgin has told you that at the end of the apparitions she will give you a visible sign that may not be needed by believers but will be useful for non-believers. Our tests have exactly the same end'.

At the end of the discussion Jakov concluded:

> 'Alright then, we will ask her this evening. You still have Sunday for your tests.'

His refusal had been so adamant that we did not hold out much hope for the answer. He did not seem disposed to changing his mind. It appeared that the answer could only be in the negative.

To our astonishment, at the end of the ecstasy on 9 June he was smiling as he rose:

> 'The Virgin answered: "You did well to ask. You can go ahead." '

19

From then on the visionaries, who had been like lions in their opposition to the tests, were as docile as lambs. friendly, cooperative and full of good humour at the annoyance caused by the complicated equipment. The Virgin's response had changed their behaviour from resistance to cooperation. We had only one day left — Sunday — and we had two sets of equipment. These were placed on Ivan and Ivanka. But the stylus on one of them must have been damaged en route and it failed to work. The other was in perfect working order.

The ecstasy began at 6.45 p.m. and it lasted 62 ± 2 seconds. It took place not in the chapel of the apparitions but in the sacristy which had more electrical outlets.

The electro-encephalogram

The electro-encephalogram indicates the rhythms of brain activity according to eight diagrams which come from the eight electrodes attached to eight different points of the skull. It is the same test as the one we carried out to study the wakefulness of drivers to discover how they slipped into sleep while driving for long periods. In the dual control vehicles the doctors who watch the curves of the graph can see the driver pass from the state of wakefulness (alpha rhythm) to the state of sleep or of dream.

It was this same test which was administered to Ivan on 10 June. It lasted for about thirty minutes, before, during and after the apparition. *During*, he is not like the driver who falls asleep. He does not sleep. He does not dream. He remains in the alpha rhythm. This is the rhythm of wakefulness and receptivity, the rhythm of the contemplative in calm prayer. (In activity or in discussion, the rhythm is beta). The rhythm which is characteristic of sleep does not show at all in the case of Ivan.

The electro-encephalogram also excludes epilepsy. Together with the clinical observation (both direct and on video) the test excludes hallucination in the pathological sense of the word. This therefore eliminates the hypothesis which the Bishop held to be certain:

> It is a question of hallucination by the visionaries and, indeed, of collective hallucination (interview of 5 September 1984, published in Italy).
>
> The events at Medjugorje are a case of collective hallucination cleverly exploited by a group of Franciscans from Hercegovina... they have manipulated the natural curiosity of the people and their profound piety towards the Virgin (P. Zanic, *La posizione attuale...* 30 October 1984, signed and sealed by the Bishop).

I was amazed to hear of this declaration being repeated by the Bishop because I recall that we had discussed the matter during a visit to Mostar. He again put forward the hallucination thesis and after some discussion dismissed the influence of the Devil, which he seemed to cling to for a while. I said:

'Hallucination is scientifically excluded by the electro-encephalogram and by clinical observation.'

The bishop had announced that he did not need our observations nor indeed did he need the visit by the doctors who had made the observations. However the commission he appointed has not to this date administered an electro-encephalogram nor has it carried out any medical studies on ecstasy.

His polemic attitude focuses on all the objections and thus he always reaches a negative conclusion; the danger is that he may also discredit the value of prayer and the apparent conversions.

The tests carried out on Pentecost Sunday were of great value in that they eliminated false hypotheses — where otherwise time would have been lost, scientific work hampered and spiritual care damaged by following avenues that lead nowhere. But we had only one test. It was necessary to have more data.

MISSION OF 6-7 OCTOBER 1984
Continuing suspense over the visionaries' refusal

Again, on Friday 5 October I arrived twenty-four hours before the doctors with a view to making arrangements for the forthcoming tests. From the moment of my arrival I began to speak with the visionaries:

'On 10 June we were able to do only one test, an electro-encephalogram on Ivan. It was necessary to verify the results of that test by checking against others in the group, and then to do further tests: blood pressure, pulse and eye examinations.'

On that day Jakov was at home suffering from measles. Ivanka objected:

'We have recently refused other doctors who wanted to do tests; it would be contrary to our prayers. If we accept there will be no end. You already have one electro-encephalogram, you want to do another today; then you will want to do others. And now still further tests. Where will it all end? we are not guinea pigs!'

'But the Virgin encouraged you to accept on June. Could you once again ask her for her opinion?'

Ivanka accepted gracefully. We hoped for a response similar to that of Pentecost. It was somewhat different:

'The Virgin said to us, "It is up to you to decide".'

What had Ivanka, Vicka and Marija decided? They had not told us and

I did not dare ask them. The Virgin had left them to choose, to exercise their freedom. Now, if they had said unambiguously that they were against the project... I would have prefered to leave the matter to their good will without any further dialogue or discussion.

Preparation for the tests
On the following day, Saturday 6 October 1984 at 3.00 p.m., Professor Henri Joyeux and his team arrived, accompanied by Dr Jacques Philippot, an ophthalmic specialist.

Electro-encephalogram, 6 October 1984
Two hours before the apparition the team set up their equipment. The visionaries were not present. Would they arrive in time for connection to the equipment? A little after 5.00 p.m., with little more than an hour to go before the ecstasy, just as the Rosary began in the church, Marija arrived. She was willing to kneel down from the beginning because the connections were short and there was no room for movement. The Professor installed seven electrodes on her. Vicka and Ivanka arrive at 5.20 p.m., about fifteen minutes before the apparition. They were attached to the other equipment (for the measurement of blood pressure and heart rhythm).

Once again the visionaries, initially opposed to the tests, had become cooperative with as much good humour as before. These tests were no pleasure: least of all for Marija who was obliged to remain immobile on her knees with wires fixed to her hair. This must have been singularly trying for a girl who had just got a diploma in hairdressing after three years of study at Mostar. After the apparition I had to lend her my comb to repair the damage.

During all of this the visionaires, though quite different one from the other, showed remarkable solidarity; they were not guided by their subjective impulses but seemed to be guided by an external direction which prevailed over their personal and collective decisions. There were, of course, subtle and unforeseeable differences — the second response of 5 October no longer represented positive encouragement but rather a kind of simple acquiescence, a *nihil obstat*, that threw them back on the exercise of their own freedom. Each one decided individually and, in contrast with their initial opposition, each became cooperative.

Eye tests
Dr Philippot began his eye tests: a study of the inner eye and tests for ocular anomalies as well as a study of their photo-motor reflexes.

—   The study of the inner eye allows one to verify the presence of pressure deep within the skull, as might be caused by a tumour. These tests, together with clinical observation, exclude all ocular anomalies (this was in contrast with the results of tests on a little blind Italian girl who had assisted at the apparition).

— The study of the photo-motor reflexes checks the functioning of the pupil. Normally it contracts in light and dilates in darkness; stronger light causes the eyelids to close (blinking). The pupil continues to react to light during the ecstasy but the doctor soon discovered that there is no blinking in the presence of bright light. Finally, Dr Philippot had brought along a screen to put in front of the eyes during the apparition. He felt some hesitation about attempting this test (which he considered almost as aggressive as the prodding test carried out by Fr Bulat).

I had advised him not to continue with the test if the visionaries seemed to react, but I believed they would not react. After all, Marija had not reacted when Dr Stopar had stood between her and the apparition and Vicka had undergone the closed eyes test without compromising the apparition.

This is exactly what happened.

The other tests which were carried out included an electro-encephalogram on Marija and an electrocardiogram on Vicka.

Tests of 7 October
On 7 October we wished to administer yet another electro-encephalogram. Ivan and Marija had already undergone this test and since Jakov and Vicka were ill, only Ivanka remained. She had always been most strongly opposed. We explained our problem to her. She knelt down calmly, ready for anything, with the same good grace and humour displayed by Ivan on 10 June and by Marija on the previous evening.

Twenty minutes before the ecstasy on Sunday 7 October there was an electrical breakdown. Breakdowns are frequent. A breakdown on the previous evening had lasted from midnight until 9.00 a.m. This was all we needed to reduce all our preparations to nothing. The suspense got worse. The recitation of the Rosary was drawing to a close. And suddenly, just a few minutes before the apparition: the lights came back!

Results of the second medical mission
Let us pull together the results of these two days of tests.

— The apparition of 6 October: 120 ± 2 seconds

— That of 7 October: 80 ± 2 seconds

These tests confirmed and completed the tests of the earlier mission.

Electro-encephalogram
The electro-encephalogram administered to Marija, before, during and after the apparition on 6 October and to Ivanka on 7 October confirmed that there was no cerebral anomaly and that there were no pathological

symptoms. The electro-encephalogram also excludes sleep, dream and epilepsy. The graphs recorded before, during and after the apparition show only minimal differences. Before the apparition, especially in Marija's case, we find the presence of the beta rhythm, the rhythm of attention and reflection, and also the alpha rhythm, indicating the state of wakefulness. This latter predominates progressively from the beginning of the ecstasy.

Electrocardiogram
The recording of the electrocardiogram and of the blood pressure show that the heartbeat remained regular (sinusoidal) before, during and after the apparition. This was the case with Vicka on 6 October and with Marija and Ivan on 7 October.

— In Vicka's case, the heartbeat accelerated during the apparition, passing from 105 beats a minute before the ecstasy to 135-140 during.

— However in Marija's case, it slowed down slightly, going from 105 beats a minute before the ecstasy to 95 during and back to 110 after.

In Ivan's case:
— before the ecstasy: from 97-111 beats per minute
— during the ecstasy: from 120-131 beats per minute
— 120 after the ecstasy (see table 00, p.00)

Eye tests
The experiment of intermittent light stimulation did not provoke any electrical discharge indicative of epilepsy before, during or after the ecstasy. On both recordings frequent eye movements are easily discernible before and after the apparition (this is also clear from the video recording), but during the apparition there is no movement of the eyeballs. This fact was an invitation to us to carry out further research into the simultaneity of the phenomenon among many of the visionaries, during a campaign planned for December 1984. The examination of the inner eye which was carried out on four of the visionaries indicates a normal state, identical before and after the ecstasy. The photo-motor reflexes (contraction of the pupil in the presence of light) are normal and unchanged before, during and after the apparition in the case of Marija and Ivanka on 6 October and in the case of Marija on 7 October.

On the other hand, the reflex of blinking in the presence of extremely strong light is absent during the apparition (Marija and Ivanka on 7 October) while it is present before and after the apparition.

Neither Marija nor Ivanka noticed the screen that was placed between them and the apparition and it did not interfere with the perception of the apparition.

This test and the others have been recorded on video and can therefore be checked by experts.

We concluded that visual perception of the surrounding world seems to disappear during the ecstasy. The visionaries' eyes remain open but seem less sensitive to light; the pupil does contract in the presence of light but there is no blinking reflex.

Refusal of 'touch' test

For the sake of completeness we should add that one of the tests which we had planned was not executed. The test in question was that of touch. The visionaries had claimed that they could touch the apparition (this is the kind of objectivity that differentiates between ecstasy and interior visions). We therefore thought of a series of tests that would provide evidence of this 'touch' phenomenon at least insofar as we could observe it from the side of the receiver. For this it would be necessary for one of the visionaries to give one or both hands to the apparition. Photographic tests would have shown the position of the hands and further tests might have revealed changes in the nervous system. But on 10 June little Jakov, who was to carry out this test (he had refused all the others), stood up somewhat confused:

'I had forgotten. And at the very time I was going to ask her the question, she disappeared.'

The same task of asking the question was given to Ivanka and Marija on 7 October, but, they said, the Virgin would not agree to it.

MISSION OF 28-29 DECEMBER

The results of the earlier tests which had been examined by several doctors at Montpellier encouraged us to go further. We planned new tests dealing with vision, hearing and larynx function.

1. Study of vision by Dr Phillippot

An electro-oculogram, which records the eye movements, had been administered to Ivan and Marija simultaneously.

— At the beginning of the ecstasy eye movements ceased almost simultaneously. This brought us back to one of the synchronisations, that of simultaneity, and also gives a strong indication of the objectivity of the apparition.

— During the ecstasy only muscular movement associated with speech was in evidence; the eyes remained immobile.

— At the end of the ecstasy eye movement reappeared, again with almost perfect simultaneity. Thus, the phenomenon of simultaneity is associated both with the ending of the eye movement and with its restarting.

2. Study of Ivan's hearing function, carried out by Dr F. Rouquerol, 29 December 1984

— Before the ecstasy the auditory pathways, which are in a healthy state, display normal conductivity. They function as far as the upper part of the brain; in other words, the auditory nerve transmits sound stimuli. Ivan reacted (jumped) when exposed to a noise of 70 decibels.

— During the ecstasy conductivity remains normal (interview of 4.6 milli-seconds between waves I and V), the same as before the ecstasy. But there was no reaction from Ivan at the onslaught of a noise of 90 decibels (equivalent to the noise of a combustion engine at high revolution) though he jumped at a noise of 70 decibels before the ecstasy. After the ecstasy he told us that he heard nothing. The cortex had not been reached.

3. Study of Ivanka's voice and larynx function, carried out by Dr F. Rouquerol, 28 December 1984

The aim of this test was to discover why and how the voices of the visionaries became inaudible at the beginning of the ecstasy. The following are the results:

1. While the visionaries recited the Rosary before the apparition the needle indicating the functioning of the larynx muscles displayed ample movement.

2. At the beginning of the ecstasy, when the voice became inaudible, the needle stopped. There was no longer any movement of the larynx. When the visionary conversed with the apparition there was movement of the lips only (articulation without phonation).

3. The needle moved again. This time the voices returned in the middle of the apparition to recite the Our Father which, according to the visionaries, had been started by the Virgin.

4. The voice disappeared in the final phase of the ecstasy as it did in the first phase (articulation without phonation).

5. The movements of the larynx reappeared at the end of the ecstasy as soon as the visionaries began to speak.

This shows that the extinction of the voice at the beginning of the ecstasy is connected with the fact that there was no movement of the larynx and, though lip movement remained normal, the act of breathing out no longer caused the vocal cords to vibrate.

Conclusion

What then is to be concluded from these tests at a medical level or from a philosophical or theological point of view? Once more we must affirm

26

that the tests only reach the receiver. However, they do allow us to describe the phenomena more precisely.

1. Synthesis of the tests and clinical observations
We might summarise the conclusions in the following way:

1. The state of ecstasy is marked by sensory disconnection from the exterior world. The visionaries do not see or hear the surrounding environment. Ivan neither hears nor reacts to a noise of 90 decibels. More precisely:

   — As far as vision is concerned, the movements of the eyeballs (looking right or left) stop during the ecstasy. The electro-oculogram administered to Marija and Ivan showed that this immobilisation of the eyeballs is virtually simultaneous. Their gaze is fixed on the apparition with an extraordinary immobility. In the case of Vicka (and sometimes Ivan) blinking of the eyelids also ceases while in the case of the others this activity is reduced by as much as half. Eye movements associated with attention to the outside world begin again at the end of the apparition, again with virtual simultaneity.

2. With regard to the hearing function, our tests showed that the auditory nerve continued to transmit sounds but that these sounds did not reach the cortex. Violent noise failed to produce a reaction and after the ecstasy Ivan confirmed that he did not notice anything. In the same way the visionaries do not feel pinching, prodding or other interventions.

   This disconnection is not total; rather it is partial and variable. During the apparition the crowds asked numerous questions. These were sometimes passed on to the Virgin by the visionaries and they sometimes relayed answers. It all happens as if the visionaries, urged on by the ecstasy (their encounter with the Virgin) gradually adapted themselves to it and eventually allowed themselves to be lost in it. At the first apparition Ivanka sees only in a vague manner and Mirjana, who resists and turns away, sees even less clearly. There is agreement between the perceptions of the outside world retained by the two visionaries and their perception of the unknown object which begins to make itself known to them. Each acts according to her powers of receptivity and initial fear. Ivanka is more receptive, Mirjana less so; in fact she resists and does not welcome the object until the second apparition. During the subsequent ecstasies the visionaries' attention is divided between the apparition and the crowds that press around them. In these conditions they retain the normal vigilance required to cope. They warn the people when they appear to annoy the Virgin or walk on her veil. Progressively, when conditions become more conducive to prayer and recollection, they enter rapidly and totally into the ecstasy and allow their perception of the outside world to disappear. Later on we will show that these variations are classic in the history of ecstasy.

3. The visionaries say that this suspension of their perception of the outside world conditions their perception of the apparition — 'of the Virgin'. Ecstasy is therefore a functional phenomenon: the weakening of their contact with the exterior world helps to strengthen the contact, of a different order, with the object (person) who appears to them.

4. The disappearance of the voice (locution without phonation) is also functional in character. It preserves the intimacy of their communication. This manifestation is connected with those already mentioned. Up to now we have not succeeded in finding a Croatian deaf-mute in order to verify the coherence of the unsounded articulations that are frequent and clear particularly in the case of Vicka and Ivanka and less so in the case of the others. (Fear of the retaliation that might follow any cooperation with the events of Medjugorje has paralysed those who might either be able to provide this service or at least have it provided.) The suspension of perception and of the voice has the same function: it preserves the intimacy of the communication between the visionaries and the Virgin who appears to them.

5. Ecstasy is a perfectly normal state and is not in any way pathological.

    —   Blood pressure and pulse are not noticeably changed (there is a slight increase or drop depending on who the visionary in question is).

    —   The facial colouring does not change. There is no evidence of that paleness which was so striking in Bernadette's case. Nor is there evidence of blushing, and this would have been somewhat disquieting as it is one of the indicators in the American system of lie detection. Dr Gabrici noted that 'there were no vaso-motrice variations in the face'.

    —   The body remains flexible and passive. When we picked up little Jakov, the lightest, he did not react. His legs remained hanging but the kneeling reflex worked perfectly when we put him back on the ground. His legs went from the vertical to the horizontal in the most natural and spontaneous fashion; this excludes catalepsy. The child is at prayer; if we try to distract him by putting him standing up he returns spontaneously to his knees.

    —   The face is perfectly at peace and relaxed. The entire appearance is one of happiness and contentment. The visionaries appear to be (and admit to being) overjoyed. Vicka's sighs express this in a most compelling manner.

28

The significant components of ecstasy are:

a. normality: there is continuity with the normal state (behaviour, pulse, blood pressure) without a break in or difficulty of transition;

b. partial disconnection from the exterior world which conditions and allows the following characteristic;

c. perception of an object (a person) which remains invisible to others and with whom the visionaries enter into a personal relationship through a receptivity which is both active and reactive.

This perception presents two contrasting characteristics:

i) To varying degrees, the ordinary mechanisms of perception no longer function. Active eyeball activity ceases; the pupil no longer reacts to light; stimuli from the auditory nerve reach neither the cortex nor the consciousness of the subject. A screen which is held up does not block out the perception of the apparition. Thus, perception is not achieved by means of the physical mechanisms of ordinary sight and hearing.

ii) However, the visionaries perceive a very real, three-dimensional person 'whom they can touch'. Their gaze is fixed on one point. They all situate the apparition in the same spot. They are influenced by her in the same way even though their individual perceptions are relatively independent. The Virgin may give a message to one without the others hearing and they can hold independent conversations simultaneously. But sometimes they receive the same surprising message together and recount it in the same manner.

This paradox is the very nerve centre of the problem:

— On the one hand the relative suspension of ordinary perceptions functionally conditions the perception of the apparition.

— On the other hand, the apparition has, for them and for witnesses, all the characteristics of objective reality despite the suspension of the ordinary modes of perception.

When these two contrasting parameters are brought together, two hypotheses emerge which go beyond the strict scientific data. The first presupposes material radiations of a different order, analogous to ultrasound. Nothing supports this hypothesis. The second hypothesis is that this perception is caused by an impact of a spiritual order (more immediate, more intuitive, without material mediation). But in this case, which seems to us the more probable, the perception has a very real existence in the appropriate areas of the brain, and involves reactions which are analogous to those of everyday life when we look, listen or speak with someone. Thus it is that this object (this person, this perception), as far as the visionaries are concerned, is not less real but rather more real than the objects of the surrounding world.

Lourdes and Medjugorje

These observations agree with the conclusions which we have reached from the study of 101 pieces of evidence on the ecstasy of Bernadette:

'From a clinical point of view', we said, 'two conclusions follow':

> On the one hand, Bernadette's ecstasy does not involve any morbid phenomenon. No fever precedes it; no peculiar behaviour accompanies it and no crisis follows; no physical or psychic trauma and no depression. Bernadette easily resumes her normal behaviour pattern, calm, simple and without any exaltation; she is perfectly at ease in what she does and in her social relationships. In this respect, her balanced attitude, her resilience, her ability to cope with even the most difficult situations have won the admiration of all, even of those who oppose her. On the other hand, the ecstasy does not appear to follow a pattern of rigorous determinism. Some days the state (of ecstasy) is very evident and on others it is not noticeable. Sometimes Bernadette is completely absorbed by the vision, while on other occasions she appears to be quite conscious of her surroundings. On all occasions she remains capable of performing that action which is most suited to the occasion. Briefly, what is happening does not appear to be the effect of a determined physical state but, in a certain fashion, transcends her physical state. It is as if the bodily ecstasy was a simple means of superior communication, the modalities of which change freely to suit the circumstances. (René Laurentin, *Lourdes, Histoire authentique des apparitions,* vol. 3, Lethielleux, pp. 133-134).

Briefly, Medjugorje displays the same coherence as Lourdes. What the collation of 101 pieces of evidence established for Bernadette, our scientific tests were able to bear out for the visionaries of Medjugorje who displayed the same fundamental characteristics, the same functional coherence, the same disconnection from the outside world (partial and variable).

The variability may be noted from the accounts of some differences:

— Bernadette's paleness struck the witnesses at Lourdes. They sometimes described it as the paleness of death. No observation of this kind was made about the visionaries of Medjugorje whose facial colour remained unchanged. As far as Bernadette is concerned, some of the witnesses exaggerated her paleness to the point of a myth. Some of the witnesses reported that her lips did not lose their colour and that her cheeks were rosy (ibid p.113, note 46, 10 pieces of evidence). It was said that Bernadette' eyes did not blink (no movement of her eyelids, p. 115, note 57). Some have also said this of the visionaries of Medjugorje. Others have said the opposite. Dr Phillippot's examination has clarified this point. During the ecstasy Ivan's and Vicka's eyes do not blink; Ivanka and Marija blink at a rate two times slower than when they are in their normal state: 10 times instead of 22 and 7 instead of 12.

— Another difference: Bernadette mirrored the greetings of the apparition. This does not appear to happen at Medjugorje though Vicka does smile. However, her smiles form part of her conversation. The alternate states of joy and sadness that were a feature of Bernadette's experience are not particularly noticeable in Medjugorje. Except in Vicka's case, there are no great changes in the faces of the visionaries and there is no great variety in their expressions. Marija and Ivan are particularly impassive (they are the more introvert by nature, just as Vicka is the more extrovert).

2. Vision or apparition?

What then of the classic question: vision or apparition? In other words, subjective or objective perception?

This question takes us beyond the realm of medicine (clinical observation or tests with scientific instruments). The question makes no sense and indeed there is no answer to it except in accordance with certain philosophical presuppositions. Those who do not worry about such things we leave to the comfort of their naiveté. There are two kinds, that naiveté which is ingenuous enough to imagine the Virgin descending in front of the visionaries like a spaceship, and a second and more critical type according to which the apparition is a subjective fabrication of the visionaries. In this latter case the coherence of the apparition remains unexplained.

A dilemma

We have already addressed the question of this dilemma (*La Vierge, apparait-elle à Medjugorje?* pp. 138-149). We regard the division as simplistic. Let us look at that knowledge which is reputed to be the most objective, our ordinary sense knowledge, knowledge of that which is intangible. I see the red apple in the green tree. The evidence is basic and incontestable. Daily and constantly we count on this. 'I have seen it' — that kind of statement cannot be rebutted. The law courts still give pride of place to 'eye witnesses'.

But even this kind of knowledge has a subjective dimension, under two headings:

1. It is the result of an impact by the object on the knowing subject. The red apple gives off vibrations which are colourless but which science can define by their rhythm and frequency. The impact of these vibrations sets off a nervous reaction which is electrical in nature and is in turn determined by physical and chemical modifications which are, of course, also colourless. This impact of the object on the body of the subject is of a *subjective* nature.

31

2. On the other hand, seeing the red apple is an act of the knowing subject and this act of the subject also has a subjective dimension.

Awareness of these subjective aspects led philosophers and scholars of the eighteenth century to declare that sense knowledge was a hallucination that was true.

This was a *reduction* of knowledge to its subjective elements. These subjective elements are functionally only the *means* to knowledge which is objective. Subjective and objective are but the two sides of the coin which is knowledge. Through our sense mechanisms we get to know the exterior world which we see. Doubts about this evidence can only derive from mental illness!

In the most objective of sense knowledge there is therefore a correlation between the *objective* and the *subjective*, of the object known and the knowing subject. The original relationship is established by two processes which are inverse and correlative: information mechanisms go from the object to the subject (centripetal movement); knowledge itself goes from the subject to the object. This movement is centrifugal. When I see a star it is not my retina, nor my optic nerve, nor the decoding system in my brain that I see, it is indeed the star. Complicated processes transmit the information to my brain which in turn decodes it, but however distant it may be, it is the star which I see. Astronomy confirms that this knowledge is soundly based.

Thus, all objective knowledge is achieved by a more or less subjective impact of the object on the subject and by a more or less subjective act of the subject which attains the object. What is proper to knowledge is that it reaches the other insofar as it is other — whether it be near or distant. This is what is known in philosophy as *intentionality*, our capacity to reach the object for its own sake. What I eat I digest and transform into my own substance. What I know, to varying degrees and according to certain limits, I know as existing in itself.

Objective and subjective are therefore not opposed. There is a kind of reciprocal conditioning. They are implied one in the other; information which is centripetal facilitates the act of knowledge (which is centrifugal), which attains the object.

We must therefore go beyond this dilemma: objective or subjective? The real problem is to discover the degree, the limits, and in what respects our knowledge is objective,and to what degree this objectivity is involved and tied up with subjective conditioning, i.e. the impact of the object and the act of the knowing subject.

This proportion is very variable. There is variety already at the level of sense knowledge, depending on each one of our senses. Vision has maximum objectivity for in it subjective sensations are reduced to a minimum.

The subjective reverberations felt by our body are greater in the case of hearing, taste, smell and sexuality (even though sexuality can and ought to be 'knowledge of the other', of man and wife, according to the biblical expression — 'Now Adam *knew* his wife and she bore...' *Gen 4: 1-25*).

Similarly, amidst the complexity of relationships and interpersonal reactions, I can really know another person. Some reduce that other person to an object, an object to be used egotistically; others reach out and know the other person as they know themselves. In passing we might note that this latter characteristic is very clearly evident in the lives of the visionaries. Even though Our Lady gives them enormous happiness, she is not for them an object of satisfaction but a person to whom they relate in a relationship of reciprocal love. Happiness comes as a bonus.

The response
Having said that, let us return to the question: is the apparition objective or subjective? In order to make sense, the question might be rephrased more precisely: what cognitional means were involved in the personal encounter of the visionaries with that person whom they call the Virgin Mary?

What complicates the answer is the fact that the means and avenues of sense perception are to a large extent unknown to us. In the case of ordinary sense perception we can observe and measure the totality of the process that takes place between the object (the red apple) and the subject; there are quantifiable vibrations and a measurable nervous influx. In the case of the apparition our tests were not able to detect any vibrations in the exterior world or any impact on the retina or the eardrum, nor were they able to detect that nervous influx which would transmit the vision of Our Lady. On this point, the eyeballs no longer manifest the ordinary movements observable in daily life, the visionaries do not hear noise level of 90 decibels, which is in fact transmitted along the auditory nerve but does not reach the brain. They hear only the voice of Our Lady.

From the point of view of objectivity there is a huge difference between:
— the six visionaries who see the Virgin as a real, three-dimensional person, whose voice they can hear and whom they can touch and,

— Helena and Mirjana who 'see in their hearts' and in this way receive interior communications.

We know that Catherine Labouré experienced these different types of perception:
— the apparition of 18-19 July 1830 would seem to have been objective and tangible;
— the vision of the medal (27 November) appeared as a two-dimensional 'painting' with the image of the Virgin on one side and the inscription on the other;

— after this Catherine experienced only interior voices, intimate and spiritual but with no accompanying vision.

The philosophical presuppositions that dominate our culture, even in clerical circles, based as they are on idealism, give great weight to the subjective element. There are those therefore who would seek to evaluate our tests in the following way: Since Dr Stopar's body or the screen held by Dr Philippot or quite simply Vicka's closed eyes (test carried out by Fr Custic, a journalist with *Glas Koncila*) did not interfere with the vision, it means that the vision is subjective. It is a product of the subject.

This conclusion does not follow. I would not deny that there are exterior radiations, ultra-sound, ultra-light. If these were present they would be of a different order of existence and we might presume that they would not be impeded by screens that are of the ordinary material order. The mere fact that others present do not see the apparition which is visible only to the visionaries in no way proves that it is a perception without an object. It simply proves that the manner of perceiving is not the same as that involved in the perception of ordinary material objects. An object from a different level of existence may well be perceived in a totally different manner. We know that certain animals, bats for example, are capable of discerning certain radiations that escape us. Other, more radically different, means of perception may well exist.

How do the visionaries see the person whom they recognise as the Virgin? It remains difficult to be precise and there is a risk of simplifying the mystery in an effort to explain this type of perception verbally. 'Through the subconscious level, i.e. a zone of the self over which the subject has no control' is the apt formula put forward by Marc Oraison *(Vraies et fausses apparitions,* Paris, 1973, pp. 133).

In summarising the results of all the tests, we are inclined towards the following hypothesis: there is real communication, from person to person and of a voluntary nature, which does not use the ordinary sensory channels (which have been suspended, disconnected, immobilised) but is achieved in a more immediate fashion at a spiritual level. However, this communication is perfectly integrated and in direct continuity with the psychic life of the visionaries; it takes a shape just as knowledge of an ordinary, three-dimensional, concrete object does. The nerve centres of the brain are involved in this act of knowing with the difference that instead of decoding from vibrations, the visonaries' impressions are received in a more immediate fashion, the nature of which we do not know. The perception by the visionaries of the person who appears, the Virgin, is not strange for them. It provokes in them normal, coherent reactions, analogous to those aroused in us when we converse with our neighbours: expression, dialogue, surprise, smiles, answers etc.

Certain simplistic hypotheses that are sometimes put forward would therefore appear to us to be forced and artificial:

— God imprints the image on the minds of the visionaries. This is meaningless to the doctor, the psychologist and, indeed, the theologian. This would not explain how this perception, which is as real and more real than any other, provokes normal reactions that fit into the ordinary scheme of things. They are aroused, they react in a fashion that fits perfectly into the continuity of their ordinary lives.

— The subconscious (its limitless possibilities are capable of supporting any hypothesis) projects subjectively an exterior perception. The normality of each person in the group, their evolution and progress run counter to this argument. Our tests would be even more radical in their exclusion of the angel theory — angels would imprint an image on the retina (Poulain). This makes little sense to an ophthalmologist and does not square with the known mechanisms of vision.

Our hypothesis — spiritual perception, which is intimate and immediate, though with normal repercussions on the organism and on the group — would seem most acceptable in the light of the two most evident facts:

— Sensory activity ceases and the interposition of a screen does not prevent the perception of the apparition.

— Numerous psychic, psychological, physiological and sociological factors demonstrate the objectivity of this perception:

1. The visionaries gaze converges on the same well-located spot. We have not been able to secure the evidence that would pin-point the spot geometrically, but the phenomenon is illustrated by a film that was shot from in front of the visionaries. For anyone who has seen the ecstasy or a photograph of it, it is evident that the visionaries look intently at the same object. On all levels, (visual, auditory, tactile) they relate in such a coherent manner to this same object that it seems impossible to explain the fact through a pre-established harmony of their subjective dispositions.

2. From the point of view of their movements it would be difficult to visualise some kind of predetermined harmony, operating from within, which would be capable of producing such coherence in their reactions, with so many instances of precise simultaneity:

   * simultaneity in kneeling without any signal or warning sign (see p. 7);

   * simultaneity of the disappearance of the voice (locution without phonation);

   * simultaneity of the re-emergence of the voice in the middle of the apparition in order to take up the recital of the Our Father, which has been started by Our Lady;

    *   simultaneity of the raising of their eyes and heads as the Virgin ascends and departs;

    *   simultaneity, precise to the second, in the cessation of eye movements at the beginning of the ecstasy and their reappearance at the end of the ecstasy in the case of the two visionaries whose tests were synchronised on 29 December 1984.

3.   The messages too are coherent despite the fact that the visionaries had independent conversations and even had different conversations simultaneously at times. There is a coherence about the secrets which they received separately according to the numbers one to ten. Even though they have not explicitly communicated them to each other, the visionaries know the object of each one of them. They refer to the secrets in code words saying, 'I have received the seventh, the eighth, the tenth secret'.

4.   This coherence struck us particularly when the visionaries, on the instruction of the apparition, changed their attitude towards the tests. As we stated already, from being vehemently opposed, they became completely cooperative. It is unlikely that the bare wall in front of them would have achieved this change of heart.

5.   From the sociological point of view, Fr Slavko Barbaric has established that this particular group, which of itself is disparate and has no leader, acts with paradoxical cohesion. The only plausible explanation of this is the apparition which had become their focal point.

6.   Add to this, at the spiritual level, the great harmony that exists between their natural and supernatural growth. These very ordinary youngsters, very like any others, 'no better and no worse', says Vicka, have attained a high degree of human maturity coupled with a degree of charity and transparent holiness that causes me to marvel more and more as the months go by. This is the real secret of Medjugorje.

7.   All the doctors who have examined or studied the ecstasy, Stopar, Madre, Botta, Joyeux, Philippot, Rouquerol, Hoarau etc., though they may use different terms, all arrive at the same conclusion: they reach a limit, and as Stopar states most explicitly, the best explanation is the transcendence of an object, which cannot be perceived through normal, material, scientific means, but whose existence nevertheless (transnormal, paranormal, whichever you wish), is certain.

Paranormal and/or supernatural

Perhaps the natural sphere of the paranormal might offer an explanation of the apparition. As yet, the scientific community has not made much progress in this area. As research has not reached any objective proofs it would be difficult to discuss the matter in the absence of definite criteria.

It is not impossible that the apparitions (at Lourdes and at Medjugorje) may well be helped by those particular predispositions which are variously called paranormal, parapsychological or mediumistic. Those who are beginning to look at the matters, which remain outside the bounds of science, tell me that Bernadette had a certain aptitude for being a medium. But if she had these aptitudes, why did they only manifest themselves eighteen times during the early months of 1858? The visionaries of Medjugorje do not give any grounds for a hypothesis along these lines. It would be hard to find a more disparate group: their ages (10-20 years), their sex (male and female), their temperaments (introvert and extrovert) and their intellectual and imaginative developments are extremely varied: Vicka, Jakov and Mirjana have lively imaginations while the imaginations of Ivan, Marija and Ivanka are somewhat duller. There is no collective conditioning on the part of the receiver. Even if the specialists in mediumism were to find certain indications in one or other of the group that they had an uptitude as a medium, other members of the group, e.g. little Jakov, a hyperactive realist or even Ivan with his lack of imagination, would offer counter-indications. As far as Medjugorje is concerned, the hypothesis of mediumism is a false trail.

I recall my conclusions concerning Bernadette, taken from *Lourdes, Histoire authentique,* vol. 2, p. 134:

> Certainly the indications in favour of the supernatural character of the ecstasy would be overstressed to the point of being elevated to the status of a probative argument. The matter is far too complex and the state of our knowledge at this time so lacking in precision, that we cannot push our study any further on this point. At least we have, at a clinical level, positive presumptions in favour of the supernatural, the essential signs of which are to be found in the moral order.

In the case of Medjugorje our scientific tests have tightened up the points of convergence and the presumptions in favour of the coherence and uniqueness of the state of ecstasy which, nevertheless, remains a challenge. Ecstasy poses a question for science to which science has no adequate answer. It notes the points of convergence but does not explain them. It reaches a limit, a threshold which it does not cross.

The point of view of the visionaries

The visionaries cheerfully cross this threshold. The apparition is simple for them. They see the Virgin. They are happy, but not with the happiness of an artificial paradise. They are left with their feet firmly planted on the ground, their faults are overcome and the best is brought out in them.

The explanation which they offer seems naive. It is however the most coherent and the most satisfying. Their encounter with God in this night-time of faith is enlightened by another encounter of a tangible nature: Our Lady, the intimate messenger of God, who shows herself freely to them. This strengthens their ties with God and with humankind. This is the secret of their authenticity, of their generosity in the face of frequent daily difficulties which they appear not to notice.

The theological point of view

If we want to bridge the gap between their naive evidence and the tests which have studied the conditioning of their receptivity, then we must do it from the same perspective as theirs, that of faith; we must use the resources of theology and mysticism which have set out the boundaries of this domain. It is the only way to understand them: from within. Otherwise the original, coherent fact is reduced to something else (play-acting, hallucination, mediumism), as has been done by opponents of the apparitions with a passion in proportion to their lack of any spirit of observation.

The question of duration

The basic theological fact to be taken into account in situating the experience of the visionaries is that the Virgin does not appear to them like a spaceship from another world. If this were the case all those present would have seen her and our tests would have yielded different results.

If the apparition is the Virgin, then, according to time-honoured Christian belief and according to the definition of Pius XII, she is with God, body and soul. The apparition could then be corporal. But the distance of this body is not measured in kilometres or in light years; it is not a question of distance in space but rather a question of duration. The Virgin belongs to God's duration — eternity. Eternity is not like time where each successive moment blots out its predecessor, a state of perpetual erosion mitigated by memory. Eternity is a simultaneous duration that gathers all things into fulness.

The 'how' of the apparition

How can a human person, who already exists in the realms of eternity, manifest herself in our time? How can space-eternity communicate with the time-space dimensions of our cosmos?

It *is* possible, in a unique way, because God's time encompasses ours. In the same way, the key to the problem lies in this transcendent duration which is beyond our ken. Here, we are touching on a mystery which goes beyond linear reasoning, verifiable and controllable by science. We may have some experience of time (disconcerting but real) but we have none whatsoever of eternity; it is beyond us to such an extent that it is difficult for us ever to consider it without dizziness.

It is not possible for our imagination to find images. Imagination sees eternity as death, while the reality is life; as a static existence rather than one ever-growing, ever-changing; as an endless flight instead of repose; as a prison, while in fact eternity confers ubiquity. Thus, while time prolongs our needs, our anguish, our hurts and our suffering, and destroys our happiness so quickly, eternity allows us to reach the height of happiness. It preserves the most valuable and profound moments of life. Eternity will reveal to us the very foundations of reality, the surface of which we have scarcely scratched, the foundation which is God.

That which persists in time as well as in eternity, is love. God himself is love. Thus the love which the Son of God manifested during the course of his earthly existence, in the crib and on the cross, continues to exist integrally in heaven. The saints were well aware of this. These events live on, as they are in themselves; eternity completes them. There is no change, no metamorphosis; instead there is persistence, the fulfilment of the best which is hidden beneath the surface here below. Thus, for believers, the crib and the cross are not an evocation of the past but are the present fulfilled in Jesus Christ, always the same, yesterday, today, eternally. Eternity gives us access, through God, to something deeper than that suspension of time so desired by Lamartine:

O time, suspend your flight
And you, propitious hours,
Suspend your course.
Let us savour the fleeting delight
of our most happy days.

Eternity does not suspend time, but gives access to the very source of time. It is the ultimate measure of time. Thus the transitory and the painful are abolished and the best is preserved. It is the duration of God himself who alone can adequately satisfy the heart of man.

The visionaries have access to Mary, who lives in God and thus they have access to God himself through this limited sign which is the apparition. Their fundamental route to God is through prayer in the night of faith. What ecstasy adds specifically to this personal encounter is that the apparition is as visible and concrete as a mother is to her child.

This visible communication is fleeting. It abolishes perception of the outside world in the same way as waking dismisses dreams. The Virgin's presence as against the ordinary, transitory, visible world extinguishes this world just as the more real takes the place of the less real. For the visionaries, this *presence* is a far more striking reality, and by comparison with it everything else is shadow.

We are now in a position to understand better why the perception of the apparition is not of the ordinary mechanical type. Thus we find our hypothesis confirmed: this communication from person to person takes place in a more spiritual, more intimate and more direct fashion with, however, the repercussions of these tangible, profound communications and dialogue being present in the centres of perception (visual, auditory) and in the various nerve networks of the visionaries. The visionaries' access to God's time has the further effect of abolishing any sense of measured time. They are unable to estimate the duration of each apparition. Whether it be long or short — from three quarters of an hour to fifty-four seconds, it is perfect, complete, satisfying and leaves them without frustration. This is one of the beautiful signs of this shared experience, of this mysterious meeting with Our Lady.

The fact that the distance between the Virgin and the visionaries is not in the order of space but rather of duration helps to resolve the fundamental paradox of the apparitions: their objective realism for the visionaries even though the ordinary sensory mechanisms of perception have not been involved. It is impossible to perceive in the same manner an object in our space-time, inserted in the materiality of our world, and a visible object which belongs to a different order of duration (space-eternity) and which is made manifest in our world without interfering with the material determinism of our world. The Virgin manifests herself in a point of our space-time dimension, without affecting it, without breaking into it as would a spaceship from a distant planet. Her localisation, though well determined as far as the visionaries are concerned, remains mysterious because the reality that frames it — a wall, an altar in the chapel of the apparitions or a police van on 1 June 1981 — disappears. This disappearance of the surrounding world, together with the disappearance of sensory perception which goes with that, demonstrates the heterogeneity of the duration of that other world. That world is God's and the Virgin belongs to it, the visionaries communicate with it in a manner that is more direct and more immediate than in the case of ordinary sensory perception.

Sign and reality

The visible apparition is not an absolute. It is a contact with the absolute, though limited and relative. Communication is made through a sign that is adapted to this world.

Though we speak of sign in relation to the apparition this by no means distances the encounter. A sign is not a screen or a veil. It is the condition for and the means of all human knowledge in this world. It is the means through which we accede to knowledge. It is not duplication; rather it is a lens through which we can see things that are otherwise invisible to the naked eye. Signs are transparent. They are infinitely rich and varied. The optics of the camera do not distance the Pope or the President filmed by the camera operator; they bring them nearer. Television networks transmit one and the same image without distorting it. It was some years before television transmitted in colour; we still do not have three dimensions, temperature, smell etc. Every sign has its limitations and its own particular characteristics. It doesn't bring us the totality of reality, merely an aspect of it.

The Virgin appears to these young Croatians with the freedom of a glorified body but in keeping with this age and its customs and ways. Sometimes Jesus is with her either as a child or suffering in his passion.

The relative nature of the apparition becomes clearer when two of the visionaries describe their 'expedition' to heaven, to hell or to purgatory. These visions, in the style of an icon, show evidence of the abstract nature, the limitation and the symbolic adaptation of the sign: white garments and fields lead one to think 'green pastures'. The receptivity of these adolescents, and the individual characteristics of each influences their reception: is this accounted for by the teaching of the Virgin or by their individual way of receiving? 'Whatever is received is received according to the measure of the receiver' (*quidquid recipitur ad modum recipientis recipitur*) according to Thomas Aquinas.

This individuality is very evident in the case of the messages. The visionaries hear them but are in no way anxious to record them verbatim in shorthand. They retain and transmit the essential. 'The Gospa said that...'. The mode of expression, which is very often indirect, carries their imprint just as each inspired book of the Bible gives evidence of its author's style.

Image imprinted by God? Or existential communication from person to person?

We must be aware of the cultural tendency of reducing knowledge to subjectivity, ecstasy to an artificial or mental product. It is one of the consequences of a culture dominated by idealism. According to this philosophy (in which all one knows is one's knowledge), the subject never attains the object (the thing-in-itself). All perception is a true hallucination since it is only the effect of material objects, of vibrations of nervous influxes that are without colour. An apparition would then be a perception without an object, or at least cut off from its object.

Through enlightening in many respects, Father Marie Eugène de L'Enfant Jesus[1] seems over-dependent on the idealist perspective in his attempts to explain the tangible perceptions of the mystics. (John of the Cross and Teresa of Avila)

> If those persons who manifest themselves really have a body, like Jesus and Mary, is it by making their real bodies tangible that they

1. Père Marie Eugène de L'Enfant Jesus, Carmelite (Henri Grialou, 1894-1967). *Je veux voir Dieu (I want to see God)*, Paris, Editions du Carmel, 1956, pp. 705-77.

manifest themselves? Exterior tangible apparitions like those with which St Bernadette or St Margaret Mary were favoured are constituted by an image which God imprints on the senses. The invisibility of the real body and the creation of the vision by the imprinting of images would explain perfectly why only one or a number of people see it while others present see only the reflection of the apparition on the faces of the visionaries.

We can therefore conclude that these extraordinary forms are produced habitually if not always by an infusion of light into the intelligence and by the imprinting of images on the senses.

What disturbs me most about this analysis is the imprinted image. Since in any case we are dealing with a mystery, why have recourse to a magician God (or indeed to juggler angels, as does A. Poulain)? What is at stake is the simple and free communication by the Virgin to these children, whatever the mysterious means of this communication. Father Marie Eugène seems nearer the right track when he says:-

In these extraordinary manifestations, the divine and the human, the transcendent and the ordinary are so admirably fused that the perfect harmony which results is itself a sign of its supernatural origin (p. 742).

We may wish to retain the terminology of scholastic philosophy, — the *species infusae* — in referring to the mediating sign through which contact is established between the knowing subject(s) (visionaries) and the object (the Virgin who manifests herself).

However, it does seem artificial and even annoying to speak of 'images imprinted on the senses by God'. This evokes some kind of duplicate projected on a screen. The opposite is true: a personal, tangible self-communication by the Virgin through spiritual means that differ from the ordinary sensory means presents less difficulty to scientific determinism and offers a better explanation of the surreal and limpid experience of the visionaries. It is of course understood that this existential knowledge takes on reality in the auditory and visual centres of the brain from which coherent responses and reactions emerge.

'The act of faith does not terminate in concepts or images', St Thomas says, 'but in reality'. The visionaries attain a reality: a real tangible person whom they meet in a more intimate and perfect way than is experienced in ordinary human encounters. Any explanation that would betray this clear experience of the visionaries would be inadequate.

The impact
Is it possible to bring any greater precision to bear on the relationship between the visonaries' experience and our tests? If knowledge presupposes an impact, where does this impact occur?

1. Is it a material impact, coming from the outside? The hypothesis cannot be absolutely excluded but there is nothing to support it. In any case this impact cannot be the same as that of our surrounding world since others present see nothing. If the radiation were to come from the outside it would no doubt be of a mysterious nature and would therefore be unsusceptible to our means of observation.

2. Does the impact take place at the level of our sensory nervous system? Our tests tend equally to exclude this hypothesis unless we are dealing with a *sui generis* impact which would, of course, remain unverifiable.

3. For these reasons our tests tend to lead us to the hypothesis of a person-to-person communication which takes place at a spiritual level, analogous to the angelic act of knowing. This knowledge obviously takes on reality in the brain. However, the vision centre in the brain does not decode sensory messages but, in an analogous fashion, interprets a more intimate message. This perception, as in the case of the perception of an ordinary object, provokes coherent reactions: dialogue, contemplation etc. for the entire duration of the apparition.

This 'more-than-real' communication is fruitful and balanced. The visionaries have a heightened and more peaceful consciousness of their identity. They have a clearer perception of their faults and they correct them. They are growing in maturity. Despite their different temperaments they understand each other perfectly without argument, sometimes in the most difficult of situations. Two of the visionaries are impulsive and by temperament more hot-headed. How is it then that they are always in agreement when secular priests and Franciscans of the diocese cannot resolve a conflict that has separated them for forty years?

The visionaries easily overcome the tensions caused by differences between them and the forceful nature displayed by some of them (Vicka and Jakov in particular), which would normally lead to an explosive situation. This perfect agreement, whatever the difficulty, is a remarkably clear illustration of the message of reconciliation.

Clarity
We should not forget the clarity of this communication which strikes the unprepared visitor so forcibly. The purity and simplicity of the ecstasy speaks for itself. For the visionaries, she is there, in front of them. The mysterious manner of their perception in no way forces us to reject the localisation of the apparition. The elimination of the surrounding realities allows them to perceive the apparition at a precise point in our space-time dimension. The visionaries themselves do not undergo any change or affectation; they suffer no distortion or morbid deformity. They remain, very simply, at their best.

The ecstasy also bears witness to another world, to which the observers — including the doctors and technicians — may be sensitive, provided they open their eyes and do not get lost in their instruments.

We have noted the multiple evidence of the striking nature of Bernadette's ecstasy at Lourdes. (*Histoire Authentique*, p. 135):

'We could see that she saw something' (Madeleine Brabazan No. 45).

'I said to myself, she is seeing something' (Marie Thardivail No. 60).

'One could easily see that it wasn't a matter of pulling faces.' (Fanny Nicolau No. 64a).

'On seeing her face, I had to think that she saw something'. (Eleonore Gesta No.34).

'Everybody had the feeling of a presence.' (Dezirat: memorandum of 2 September 1878).

'If you had seen her face during the apparition you would have said that she was herself the Virgin.' (Andre Sajous, ibid. p. 136).

A number of witnesses see Bernadette in ecstasy as an image, a reflection of Our Lady. The same expressions recur spontaneously at Medjugorje in the presence of the kaleidoscopic multiplication of the six very different visionaries. However, this transparency, which each person feels in proportion to the degree of his or her sensitivity, leads us beyond the realm of the measurable, beyond the scope of the scientific tests. Let those understand who can understand. Our instruments can only take you to a threshold beyond which they lose touch.

Synthesis

To conclude on these medical, psychological and spiritual analyses:

1. The apparitions are not sleep or dream or hallucination in the medical or pathological sense of the word. This is scientifically excluded by the electro-encephalogram and by clinical observation. (Despite widespread false statements carried by the world press). Professor Emilio Servadio in *Tempo*, 9 December 1984, underlines the fact that this expression of collective hallunication is a contradiction in terms, a psychiatric clanger.

2. Ecstasy is manifested as a functional state in which ordinary sensory perception is suspended for the benefit of a visible perception of a person. This does not interfere with the determinism of this world and does not upset the lives of the visionaries into whose existence the ecstasy is inserted harmoniously and without difficulty.

3. The ecstasy is not pathological, it is a coherent state that is beneficial to the visionaries. It does not diminish their identities nor lessen their

differences. It fulfils them and elevates these ordinary adolescents ('neither better nor worse than anyone else') to a human and spiritual level that is remarkable in difficult conditions and is a cause of universal admiration (apart from those observers whose sole aim is to find lies and contradictions in the visionaries' spontaneous and ingenuous proposals — see our study, *Autopsie des fausses nouvelles* (*Autopsy of false news*)).

4. The conclusions clearly show that we are dealing with a perception which is essentially objective both in its causality and in its scope: this does not exclude the element of sign which is inherent in all human knowledge, nor does it exclude the limits and peculiarities of a given sign tailored to the measure of the receiver. Just as the ordinary world is more real than the world of dreams, so too the Virgin is more real for them than is the ordinary world; she is not *unreal* but, rather, *surreal*. She does not belong to our space-time dimension; she can insert herself into this dimension without interfering with its limitations because she belongs to another type of duration, the eternity of God.

5. The ecstasy has the effect of transferring the visionaries into another special duration, a duration that is *sui generis*, that differs from our realm of time as measured on the clock. They lose contact with this latter dimension. They are lost in prayer. Thus they reach their fulfilment in these brief moments during which profound links between them and God and the communion of saints are forged.

6. The labels used to explain or, indeed, to explain away ecstasy — hallucination, the emergence of the unconscious etc. — explain nothing and contradict scientific observation. Science has no means of identifying the object of the apparition and honestly defines the limits beyond which it cannot go. The most obvious answer is that given by the visionaries who claim to meet the Virgin Mary, Mother of God.

7. The negative nature of the sensory examinations carried out during the ecstasy and the coherent reactions of the visionaries impose the hypothesis of a spiritual — and real — communication, from person to person. This perception, which is achieved through means that differ from those of ordinary perception, manifests an individual and collective coherence and the characteristic of objective reality at the level of the perceptions and reactions that flow from it.

8. Catholic theology underlines the particular nature of the phenomenon: each fact is different in the history of the Church and the communion of saints through the relativity of a sign given within the limitations of space and time. The criteria used to discern these phenomena and those associated with the mystical experience would tend to confirm

that the children's experience has as its object she whom they recognise and to whom so much good gives witness.

MEDICAL EVALUATION OF PROFESSOR JOYEUX AND HIS TEAM
I Historical account and objectives of the study
A. History
At the beginning of March we read through René Laurentin's book, *La Vierge, apparait-elle a Medjugorje?* (OEIL). We were intrigued but not convinced. Nevertheless, on 20 March at 8 a.m. we telephoned René Laurentin who informed us of his desire to put together a medical team to carry out a scientific examination of these extraordinary phenomena, which were in danger of coming to an end without any medical examination having been carried out.

The historical unfolding of the undertaking is described at the beginning of this book: one journey to prepare the ground and three further trips to administer the tests, which were completed from 24 March to 30 December 1984.

Our first impressions of the visionaries (24-25 March) are worth noting: Vicka, Ivan, Marija and Jakov are like any other youngsters of their age. We saw no signs of hallucination, pretence or invention. They were calm, serene and deeply serious and did not play at being celebrities. They remained normal in all the circumstances in which we observed them. They did not collude with each other either before, during or after the essential event of their day, and they all returned home to their families.

These young Yugoslavs are easy to communicate with (even in the case of strangers, a doctor and an engineer); they allow themselves to be photographed or filmed but they do not seek this out; rather, they appeared to be somewhat annoyed by all the fuss that surrounded them. They are country youngsters who do not appear to need either a psychologist or a psychiatrist. They dress in the normal fashion of other young people of their country. They give no impression of being bigoted, each seeming to have his or her own personality; we felt at ease with all of them: they are neither geniuses nor simpletons; they are not being manipulated but remain free and healthy in mind and body.

B. Necessity for a scientific study
The impossibility of reaching the vision (the transmitter) obliges scientists to study the receivers, i.e. the visionaries themselves.

1. Three essential questions
Three essential questions are inevitably raised for any scientist confronted by these phenomena.

Are their psysiological functions modified during the ecstasy and if so, in what way?

— brain function
— eye function (motor and reflex)
— heart function
— hearing function
— voice function (phonation)

Perhaps we are dealing with collective deceit? Would not a lie detector eventually unmask such deceit? In facing up to these three questions our team was conscious of a number of handicaps which are important to define.

2. Difficulties of execution

Our first weakness lay in our total ignorance of the Croatian language. There was no avoiding this. The young people spoke only their mother tongue. We used a number of unofficial interpreters (four or five in succession). These were unofficial in the sense that they were not nominated by either the local civil or ecclesiastic authorities. They understood either Italian, German or English, all languages that members of the team understood to varying degrees.

The distance of 1800 km between Medjugorje and Montpellier involved long journeys. Professional obligations and the difficulties of going through administrative formalities — that might in any case not have had a successful outcome — dictated short, repeated studies that could be undertaken over the forty-eight hours of a weekend. However, this arrangement allowed us to undertake two complete studies during each mission, since the apparitions took place every day. We planned our departure from the university to allow us to arrive in Medjugorje in the early afternoon after a twenty-four hour journey. This gave us sufficient time to set up our equipment.

The equipment: during our first mission, 24-25 March, the sacristy was chosen as the most suitable location for the tests in preference to the chapel of the apparitions, as only there were there sufficient electrical sockets. Transporting the equipment across the various borders, especially in Yugoslavia, was easy. The important thing was that each item was brought out again so that there would be no suspicion of trading.

C. How could the scientific programme be established?

1. Previous medical examinations, summarised earlier in this book by Fr Laurentin (pp. 11-27), were collated.

2. There was very little bibliographical information available on these extraordinary phenomena. In fact, no scientific medical study of similar

cases had been carried out, either at Lourdes, La Salette (one apparition in 1866) or Pontmain (one apparition in 1871). On-line queries to international bibliographical data bases had yielded such key words as deception and lie detection. The bibliographical references which we obtained and subsequently used could be summarised as follows: cardio-vascular, respiratory, cutaneous and physiological changes used in the detection of lies through polygraphic recording are not reliable. In fact there is no difference of a statistically significant nature in the results obtained from both cheating and non-cheating subjects (*Journal of Personality & Social Psychology,* 1981, 40, 1118-25). The same was true of recordings of voice levels — tone (*ibid*, 1977, 35, 345-50). An electrical study of the cutaneous reaction to an emotional state (by recording the electrical resistance of the dermis) can be made but does not give definitive answers to the question: Is there or is there not deceit? The net result merely indicates 'embarrassment' of the subject, the fact that the subject is ill at ease, in a 'state of contradiction' or simply in an 'emotional state' (*Biological Psychology*, 1982, 14, 213-8).

Hypnosis may be of some help when the subject is willing to undergo hypnosis. As a method it is, however, still incomplete, as a well-prepared subject may, even under hypnosis, give false information. Thus both internal and external factors could give rise to contradictory results (*Ann. New York Academy of Science*, 1980, 347, 73-85). The research programme which we put together therefore aimed at a clinical and para-clinical study of the visionaries of Medjugorje before, during and after the apparition, from the point of view of differences in the functioning of their principal receptive organs: brain, vision, hearing, voice and, in particular, the vegetative cardiac functions.

Our programme therefore took into account the psychiatric and psychological studies undertaken by our Yugoslav colleagues (more competent judges will decide eventually on the possibility of a clinical anomaly of a neuropsychiatric nature) and, equally, the absence of scientific studies of such phenomena.

II Authors of the study

All the members of the team are graduates of the faculty of medicine of the University of Montpellier and live in the city or its suburbs. All practice medicine either in public hospitals or privately.

Dr Henri Joyeux, born 28 June 1945, who was team coordinator, is Professor of Cancerology in the Faculty of Medicine at Montpellier. He is a hospital surgeon in the Cancer Institute of Montpellier and is director of a laboratory which researches nutrition and is involved in experimental cancerology.

Dr Jacques Philippot, born 10 July 1945, former hospital intern, has a diploma in ophthalmology and is consultant to hospitals in Montpellier. He undertook the study of the ocular and visual functions.

Dr Francois Rouquerol, born 30 October 1947, has a diploma in otorhinolaryngology (ear, nose and throat); he is a former head of clinic at the faculty and expert law-court witness and was responsible for the study of the functions of hearing and voice.

Dr Bernard Hoarau, born on 4 September1933, Assistant clinic head in the cardiology department of the University Hospital. He interpreted the recordings of the electro-cardiagram, blood pressure and heart rhythm.

Dr Jean Cadhilhac has been a member of the Yugoslav Society of Neurophysiology since 1970. He was consultant and interpreter of all the neurophysiological aspects and studied the different video recordings of the ecstasies at Medjugorje.

René Dubois-Chabert, born 13 April 1938, is an electrical engineer. He was responsible for the technical operation of the tests.

III Clinical and para-clinical study

A. Subjects studied
Jakov Colo, born 6 March 1971 at Bijakovici, attends the local village school.

Ivan Dragicevic, born 25 May 1965 at Bijakovici.

Ivanka Ivankovic, born 25 June 1965, is a student at Mostar.

Vicka Ivankovic, born 3 September 1964, at Bijakovici, is a student at the professional College of Textiles at Mostar (she is not related to Ivanka Ivankovic).

Marija Pavlovic, born 1 April 1965 at Bijakovici, has just completed three years professional training as a hair-stylist at Mostar.

The clinical and para-clinical studies were administered thirty minutes to one hour before the ecstasy, during the ecstasy, and from ten to fifteen minutes after the ecstasy.

B. Chronology of the medical missions
First mission: 24-25 March 1984
This was a purely clinical study of Vicka, Ivan, Marija and Jakov.

Second mission: 9-10 June 1984
9 June, a purely clinical study of Jakov, Ivan and Marija. 10 June, clinical and para-clinical studies of Jakov, Ivan, Marija and Ivanka.

On the same day two electro-encephalographic recordings were made of Ivan and Marija and one recording of heart rhythm and blood pressure of Ivanka.

Third mission: 6-7 October 1984
6 October, a clinical and para-clinical study of Vicka, Marija and Ivanka were carried out.

An electro-encephalographic recording of Ivanka was made in conjunction with a recording of heart rhythm and blood pressure. An ophthalmic study of each of the visionaries was undertaken before, during and after the ecstasy.

7 October, Marija, Ivanka and Ivan were examined — clinical and para-clinical examinations: recordings of heart rhythm and blood pressure in the case of Ivan, and an ophthalmic study of each of the visionaries. A video recording was made before, during and after the ecstasy on each day.

Fourth mission: 28-29 December 1984
28 December, Jakov, Marija, Ivan and Ivanka were examined clinically and para-clinically. Simultaneous recordings of Ivan's and Marija's eye movements were made. A study of the movements of Ivanka's larynx was completed.

29 December, Marija and Ivan were examined clinically and para-clinically and recordings were made of Ivan's evoked auditory potentials. Again a video recording was made before, during and after the ecstasy on each day.

C. Duration of the ecstasies studied
It was possible to record the precise duration of only five of the ecstasies:

10 June	62 $\pm$ 2 seconds
6 October	102 $\pm$ 2 seconds
7 October	80 $\pm$ 2 seconds
28 December	65 $\pm$ 2 seconds
29 December	85 $\pm$ 2 seconds

D. Clinical remarks
1. Descriptive account
We will move immediately to a synthesis, the summary in the preceding chapter of the early clinical observations and the unfolding of the four missions.

2. Synthesis
Behaviour before the ecstasy
(a) Behaviour identical to that of other young people: What is most striking is the total absence of a difference in the behaviour of these young people

from that of others of the same age, the same country or even from other countries. We had many opportunities to make comparisons between them and their contemporaries. Many members of the medical team found it difficult to pick them out as they saw them enter the room of the apparitions for the first time.

(b) Seriousness, simplicity and natural reserve. It is their seriousness — although not excessive — and their simplicity which are their strongest characteristics. In fact, we never noticed any attempt at affectation, pretentiousness or complexity, nor was there anything far-fetched in their behaviour.

Each of them gives indications of a natural reserve almost approaching timidity, which tends to make them keep to themselves but which disappears when they get to know the questioner and grow in confidence.

(c) Different character traits. Apart from the common characteristics described above each one displays his or her own character traits (in behaviour).

Jakov Colo, who was 13 in March 1984, is as impulsive, roguish and wild as any youngster of his age. We saw a change in him between March and June. He appeared to become more responsible. It was he who first had the idea of asking Our Lady's opinion on the test we wished to undertake.

Ivan Dragicevic, who was 19 in May 1984, is a very reserved young man, almost solitary; he likes sport (some of the team played football with him); he answers questions precisely, appears to reflect a good deal and tends towards introspection. He refused very firmly to answer a precise question about his future; 'it is his private life and nobody else's business'.

Marija Pavlovic, who was 19 in April 1984, is a calm young girl, open and smiling. She is discreet and keeps to the background but is at the same time positive and reassuring in dealing with questioners. One feels that she has enormous inner reserves.

Ivanka Ivankovic, who was 18 in June 1984, has regular features and the assured walk and deportment of a student closely in touch with her times; she is accessible, sympathetic and open, but does not lack strength of character.

Vicka Ivankovic, who was 20 in September 1984, is the most open and smiling of the group. Her angular features, her piercing gaze, her strong voice, all combine to give her a particular character; she is extrovert, her approach is simple and direct and she is incapable of hiding her feelings.

All of these young people appear normal, well-balanced and healthy in mind and body.

Behaviour during the ecstasy
Our observations during the eight ecstasies at which we assisted did not

allow us to note any behavioural differences in the visionaries. Only in the case of Jakov were we able to notice a certain growth in maturity between 25 March and 10 June. He had just had his thirteenth birthday on 6 March and we had not known it. He had appeared somewhat downcast and almost dumb during the March ecstasies. In June he was more cooperative and more concerned, like his companions.

The most striking features of the behaviour of the five during this period are certainly their receptivity, their attention and their way of looking at a particular point, all of which indicate a state of relationship. In fact, each one of them appeared simultaneously and successively, to receive information from and to converse with a person whom we as doctors have never seen. Some of the visionaries, more expressive than others, in particular Vicka and Ivanka, 'speak' more than Marija, Ivan and Jakov.

Behaviour after the ecstasy
There is very little difference in the behaviour of each of the visionaries, though each one retains his or her particular characteristics. The ecstasy does not inhibit them; it simply makes them happy; they are fulfilled. After Mass Jakov thinks of joining his friends for play or simply going home, Ivan remains serious and solitary, distancing himself as much as possible from the crowd which, at all costs he tries to avoid; Marija awaits the end of the ceremonies in order to fold away the vestments of the many concelebrants. Ivanka and Vicka are more approachable and are happy to be greeted by the many strangers they meet.

3. Complementary study of the video recordings
Numerous video recordings were carefully analysed by the medical team, joined by two neurophysiologists from the university:

— On 5 April a video was shown. It was produced in English, by David Carver of the St Francis Association for Catholic Evangelisation, under the title *The Path of Peace*. A number of videos were recorded between 1983 and 1984 by Fr René Laurentin and were produced by ENES Video Publishers.

— An in-depth report by Jean-Claude Darrigaud, Senior Reporter with Antennes 2, ENES Video Publishers.

— A recording of the 'pricking test' on Vicka carried out by a member of the episcopal commission.

— The recordings made by our own team on 6 and 7 of October, and on 28 and 29 December 1984. The recording (with camera face-on to the visionaries) made by Mr Engelbert of Brussels on 28 December 1984.

E. Conclusions of the clinical studies

The clinical study of the visionaries before, during and after the ecstasy, allows us to eliminate formally all clinical signs comparable to those observed during individual or collective hallucination[1], hysteria, neurosis or pathological ecstasy.

1. There are no clinical signs of individual or collective hallucination

Collective hallucinations are normally encountered among drug addicts; they are the classical signs among users of hashish and other hallucinogens. The behaviour of the young visionaries, before, during and after the ecstasy allows us to eliminate individual hallucination. In fact, the circumstances surrounding the apparition are not at all similar to those observed during the course of real hallucinations in a normal subject. In a sick patient hallucinations are most common at the moment of waking or going to sleep. In the case of the visionaries at Medjugorje, their daily 'meeting' takes place at 5.45 p.m. in the winter and 6.45 p.m. in the summer — always the same time — and is not, therefore, associated with waking or sleeping which is, in any case, excluded by the electro-encephalogram. There is no tactile hallucination.

None of the visionaries feels sensations arising from burning, pricking etc. Hallucination is not induced by any of them: their attendance pattern is not regular, any of them may be absent due to school, illness, hospital... There were times when only one visionary was present and this was not always the same one. We did not observe hallucinatory type behaviour in any one of the visionaries.

2. There is no individual or collective hysteria

Hysteria is the most widespread of nervous conditions. Its most obvious characteristic is suggestibility. The hysterical subject is extremely open to influence; the observer is struck by the psycho-plasticity of the subject's psychic makeup, his or her inconstancy and changeability. Hyper-expressivity is another dominant trait; behaviour is theatrical with excessive and superficial emotional demonstrations. The hysterical person tries to seduce and 'move' people at all costs. He is afraid of displeasing and will change or adapt his attitude to suit another person. There is always an astonishing degree of emotional immaturity coupled with a childish

---

1. The *Concise Oxford Dictionary* defines hallucination as 'apparent perception of external object not actually present' which might fit the case of Medjugorje if *a priori* one held that an object from another world does not exist or if one understands 'not actually present' in a purely empirical way. Medically speaking 'hallucination' indicates a pathological state and it would appear to us that use of the word should be restricted to psychiatric illness.

egocentricity. The hysteric continuously falsifies the elements of his existence. Hysterics complain constantly of insurmountable debility and have almost permanent problems associated with diet (bulimia, irregular eating patterns). None of these indications were observed in the visionaries either in our study of the videos or through direct clinical examination.

3. There is no neurosis

The symptoms of neurosis are almost infinitely variable: Mental (anxiety, hyper-emotionalism, inhibition, obsession, phobia, depression, personality disorder), physical (various pains, spasms, vertigo, debility etc.). The visionaries have no symptoms of anxiety or obsessional neurosis, phobic or hysterical neurosis, hypocondriac/or psychosomatic neurosis, and there is no indication of any psychosis.

We can make these formal statements in the light of detailed clinical examinations.

4. There is no catalepsy

In the case of catalepsy there is complete suspension of voluntary muscular movement leading to complete immobilisation; assumed positions are retained and there is no capacity for spontaneous movement. All gesticulation ceases. This phenomenon has not been observed in the visionaries who quite naturally drop to their knees together when, as they say, they see Our Lady. They remained quite naturally in the kneeling position while the medical team were carrying out their tests; rather than freezing, the muscles governing gesticulation remain relaxed. The visionaries move spontaneously and without the slightest difficulty right from the end of the ecstasy. During the ecstasy they are not in a state of catalepsy, but in a state of prayer and peaceful contemplation.

5. It is not a pathological ecstasy

Immobility is a characteristic of pathological ecstasy as are sensory inaccessibility and expressions of sublime joy (in the case of the visionaries the muscles governing gesticulation and the voice function during certain periods of the ecstasy). Pathological ecstasy can be observed in the cases of pathological mystics, hysterics, the chronically delirious and those suffering from hallucinations. They generally present a web of religious and erotic preoccupations. Ecstasy alternates with excesses of exaltation and lewd excitability although the subjects remain useless in the face of practical activity. What would appear to happen is 'a process of compensation which corresponds to intellectual or emotional insufficiency' (Th. Kammerer in Dr Porot, *Manuel de psychiatrie,* 'Extase').

None of these signs or preoccupations is present in these young people whom we have examined carefully. We were able to see them, before an apparition, dealing with a handicapped girl whom they did not know. We were able to speak freely with them with the help of one or more interpreters; we witnessed their reactions to foreign newspapers in which they were portrayed as being mentally ill... in all these circumstances their behaviour remained normal and calm. The daily ecstasy does not excite them, does not constrain them, does not make them ill and does not give them a false sense of pride.

F. Electro-encephalographic functions
Electro-encephalographic recordings were made of:

> Ivan Dragicevic, 10 June 1984
> Marija Pavlovic, 6 October 1984

In both cases the equipment used was Alvarelectronic-Reega Minihuit-TR. The micro-voltage was 50, running at 15mm/sec, the electrodes connected, 1-2,2-3,4-5,1-13,3-13,4-14,6-14. The electrodes were positioned as follows: 1 right frontal, 4 left frontal, 2 right parietal, 5 left parietal, 3 right occipital, 6 left occipital, 13 right temporal, 14 left temporal. During both examinations the intermittent light tests were also administered.

1. Electro-encephalogram on 10 June (Ivan)
The recording was made for one minute before the apparition, during the 62 $\pm$ 2 seconds of ecstasy and then for one minute after the apparition.

Interpretation
The graph is overlaid with details relating to the subject's perspiration, the recital of the Our Father, and the opening and closing of his eyes. The normal electrical activity associated with wakefulness, type alpha at 11 cycles/sec, is clearly identifiable; it is symmetric on the right and left longitudal derivatives, before, during and after the apparition.

The examination shows no sign of sleep or of epileptic discharge.

2. Electro-encephalogram on 6 October (Marija)
Interpretation
The graph is normal. To be noted: before the ecstasy there were periods of alpha type rhythm (10 cyles/sec) and periods of heightened attention with the more rapid beta type (20 cycles/sec). During the ecstasy we observed a period of attention with initially rapid rhythms, then the reappearance of alpha type, synchronous and almost continuous during a long period of 65 seconds. After the ecstasy the beta rhythm returns with intermittent and less continuous presence of alpha type.

Conclusion
Both electro-encephalographic studies allow us to conclude:

PRE-ECSTASY

880941

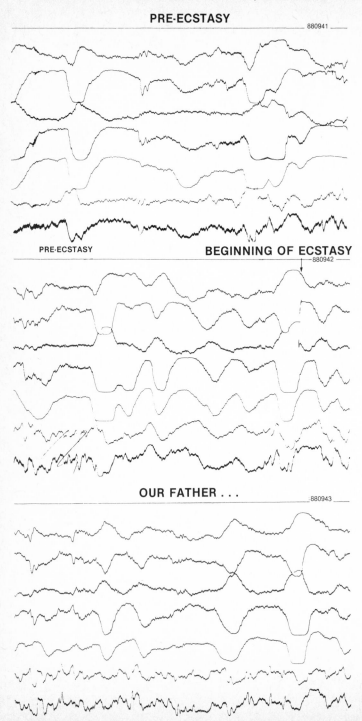

PRE-ECSTASY   **BEGINNING OF ECSTASY**

880942

OUR FATHER . . .

880943

HE SPEAKS

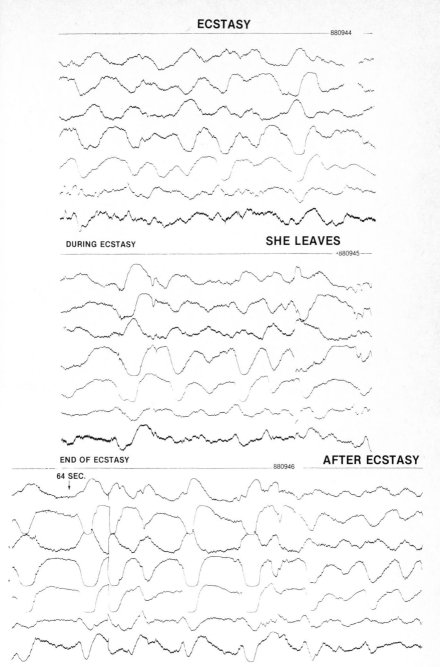

ECSTASY

880944

DURING ECSTASY   SHE LEAVES

880945

END OF ECSTASY   AFTER ECSTASY

880946

64 SEC.

Before the ecstasy: a mixture of beta rhythm (reflection: 20 cycles per second) and alpha (attentive).

During the ecstasy: pure alpha rhythm (rhythm of wakefulness) — neither sleep nor dream.

ELECTRO-ENCEPHALOGRAM OF MARIJA, 6 October 1984

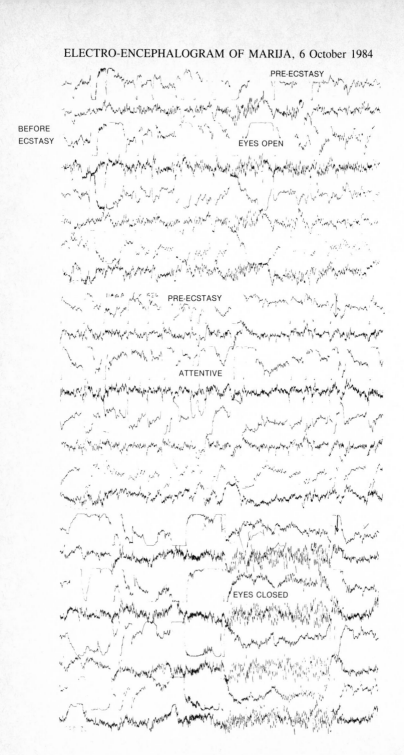

PRE-ECSTASY

BEFORE
ECSTASY

EYES OPEN

PRE-ECSTASY

ATTENTIVE

EYES CLOSED

DURING THE ECSTASY: Pure alpha rhythm

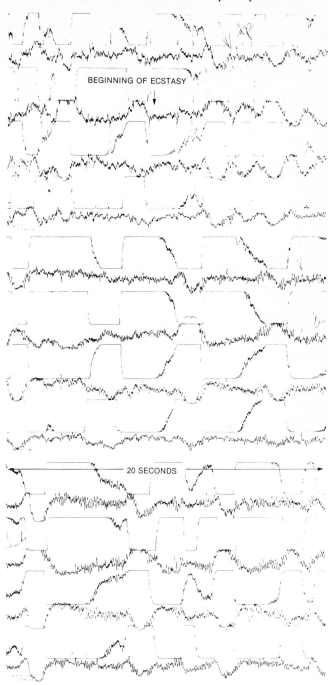

BEGINNING OF ECSTASY

20 SECONDS

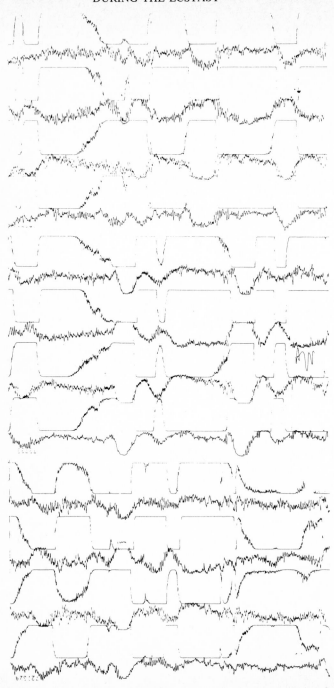

END OF ECSTASY AND AFTER ECSTASY

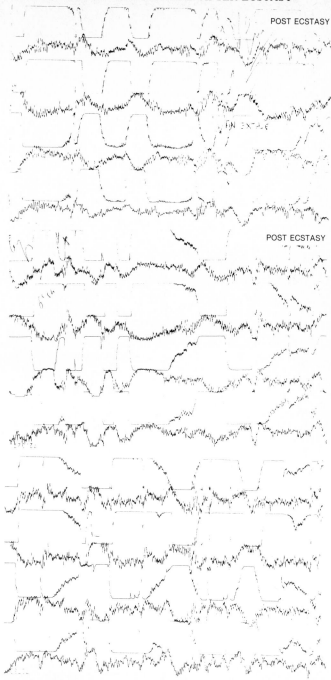

POST ECSTASY

FIN EXHALE

POST ECSTASY

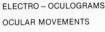

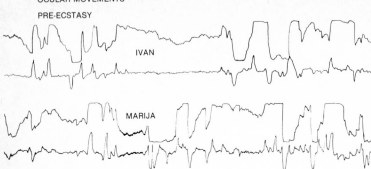

IVAN

MARIJA

PRE-ECSTASY 28 December 1984

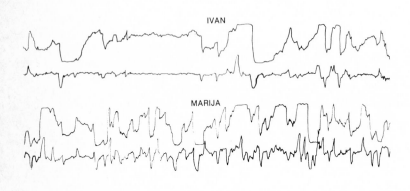

IVAN

MARIJA

SIGN OF THE CROSS

IVAN

SPEECH

4 SECONDS

CESSATION OF

OCULAR MOVEMENT

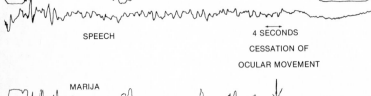

MARIJA

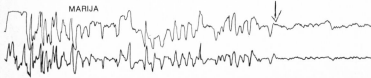

ECSTASY 28 December 1984

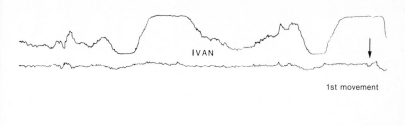

IVAN

1st movement

MARIJA

205948

POST-ECSTASY 28 December 1984

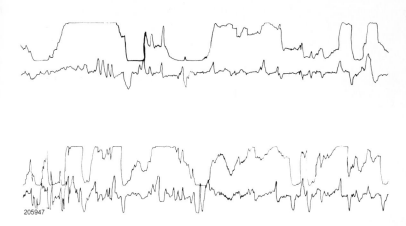

205947

Simultaneous electro-oculograms of Ivan and Marija, 28 December 1984: before and after the ecstasy. The eye movements cease simultaneously to the nearest second.

63

1. Ivan Dragicevic and Marija Pavlovic have normal and identical electro-encephalograms, before, during and after the period of ecstasy.

2. The electro-encephalograms allow us to exclude totally the existence of the phenomena of dreams, sleep or epilepsy, in both subjects, on the day of the tests.

3. Intermittent light stimulation during three recordings showed no electrical discharge of an epileptic type before, during or after the ecstasy.

G. Ocular and visual function

This function was studied by Dr Jacques Philippot during the third and fourth medical missions.

1. Tests completed

— Examination of the back of the eye before the ecstasy.

— Photomotor reflexes (contraction of the pupil in the presence of light) before, during and after the ecstasy.

— Blinking reflex (closing the eyelids) when something approaches or by being dazzled. We used a strong naked light.

— Comparative study of frequency of blinking, before, during and after the ecstasy, for a period of identical duration.

— 'Screening test' for Ivanka and Marija which consisted in placing a sheet of opaque cardboard before their eyes during the ecstasy.

— Study of the mobility of the eyeballs, before, during and after the ecstasy by electro-oculographic recording, simultaneously administered to two visionaries.

2. Results

— Examination of the back of the eyes of Marija, Ivanka and Vicka on 6 October and of Marija, Ivanka and Ivan on 7 October were normal and were identical before and after the ecstasy.

— Direct and conscious photomotor reflexes (the simultaneous symmetric reflexes of both eyes to light) are normal and symmetric before, during and after the ecstasy for Ivan, Marija and Ivanka on 7 October.

— The reflex of blinking at dazzling light is absent during the ecstasy for Marija and Ivanka on 7 October while it is present both before and after.

— During the ecstasy the number of eyelid movements is clearly less than the number observable before or after. Vicka and Ivan had no eyelid movement.

Number of Blinks per minute	Before the Ecstasy	During the Ecstasy	After the Ecstasy
Vicka 6 October	3	0	4
Ivanka 7 October	22	10	28
Marija 7 October	12	7	14
Ivan 7 October	14	0	13

Number of eyelid blinks per minute of four of the visionaries, before, during and after the ecstasy on 6 and 7 October (study of video recording).

Interpretation of simultaneous electro-oculograms on Ivan and Marija
— At the beginning of the ecstasy Ivan's and Marija's eye movements ceased simultaneously almost to the second.
— During the ecstasy the only movements recorded were muscular and related to gesticulation and speaking when they communicate with the person whom they see. Their eyes remained immobile.
— After the ecstasy the eye movements and the muscular movements of the face began again simultaneously to the second.

The graphic recording of the simultaneous movements of the eyeballs in the case of Marija and Ivan on 28 December indicates simultaneity to the second in the cessation of movement at the beginning of the ecstasy and again, simultaneity to the second in the return of movement at the end of the ecstasy. The 'screen test' during the ecstasy did not change Marija's or Ivanka's behaviour on 7 October; after the ecstasy they said that their vision of Our Lady was not impaired and that they did not see the screen in front of them.

The study of the video made by M. Englebert on 28 December shows that their gaze converges (on one point).

Conclusion
The normality of the results of the examination of the back of the eye excludes any organic anomaly (either ocular or cerebal, whether due to swelling or not).

Visual hallucination caused by damage to the sensory receptor and the surrounding area (often found among the elderly and sick) is excluded.

The ocular system is anatomically and functionally normal.

Ecstasy does not suppress the functioning of the reflex of the pupil.

During the ecstasy the functioning of the eyelid reflex to threat or dazzling light is inhibited. Regular physiological blinking of the eyelids is less frequent in two of the visionaries and is totally absent in two others.

At the beginning of the ecstasy there is a simultaneity to one-fifth of a second in the cessation of eyeball movement which begins again simultaneously at the end of the ecstasy.

A screen placed before the visionaries' eyes does not impair their vision. Their gaze converges on the same point.

H. Cardiac function
The results were interpreted by Dr Volpilière.

1. Tests carried out
We completed electrocardiograph recordings of the blood pressure and heart rhythm before, during and after the ecstasy, using a Siemens Cardiostat 701.

2. The results
The electrocardiograms of 6 and 7 October permit us to affirm that the heart contraction is normal and regular (sinusoidal). The heart rhythm was calculated from the graphs of the electrocardiogram and by recording with a blood pressure armlet.

Pulsations per minute	Before Ecstasy	During Ecstasy	After Ecstasy
Ivanka 10 June 1984	144	125	136
Vicka 6 October 1984	104	140-135	145
Marija 7 October 1984	105-95	99-95	110
Ivan 7 October 1984	111-107-97 successive measures	131-120 successive measures	120

Number of pulsations per minute of four of the visionaries.

Blood Pressure	Average blood pressure undergoes changes during the ecstasy:		
	Before Ecstasy	During Ecstasy	After Ecstasy
Ivanka 10 June	152	138	123
Ivan 7 October	123	112	125

Average blood pressure in millimetres of mercury measured with a Critikon-Dynamap-Tm

ELECTROCARDIOGRAM OF VICKA, 6 October 1984

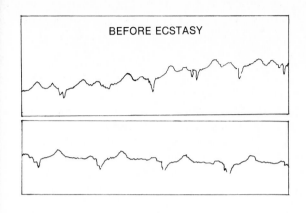

Before ecstasy:
Heart rhythm of
104 beats per minute.

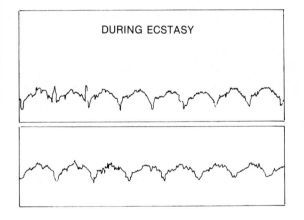

During ecstasy:
Heart rhythm of
135 beats per minute.

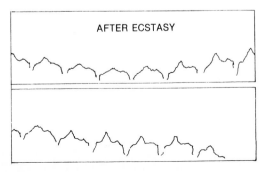

After ecstasy:
Hearts rhythm of
145 beats per minute.

Heart contraction is normal and regular (sinusoidal) during the ecstasy. The rhythm increases and remains high for the minute following the ecstasy.

Conclusion

— During all phases of the study the heart rhythm appears rapid, always remaining above 90 pulsations.

— During the ecstasy proper there is a slight drop in Ivanka's and Marija's heart rhythm while there is a slight acceleration in the heart rates of Vicka and Ivan.

These results are not significant. They indicate a difference in emotional behaviour if one admits — and it is probable — that the ecstasy period, including preparation and the time immediately following, represents an event that is always new and paranormal for the visionaries.

Changes in the blood pressure of two of the visionaries, one at a fairly rapid rhythm and the other at a slower rhythm during the ecstasy, with a mercury drop from 4 to 11mm are not significant.

I. Auditory Functions

Study of this function was completed by Dr François Rouquerol during the fourth mission.

1. Two questions were raised:

a. Are the visionaries' sensory receptors normal?

b. How do the auditory pathways work during the ecstasy since the visionaries claim to hear a female voice, which nobody else hears? Are we dealing with an auditory hallucination?

An essential test was an objective study of 'evoked auditory potentials'. This study is used:

a. in the case of children to discover deafness from birth, thus enabling re-education to begin early;

b. in the case of adults to detect deceit in those claiming to be hard of hearing.

2. Technical aspects of the study

The equipment used was PEA 1010 (RACIA). This is a modern electrophysiological study which determines the conductivity of the eighth cranial pair. (There are in fact twelve cranial pairs and the eighth represents the left and right auditory nerves.) The test was administered to Ivan during the ecstasy of 29 December. The ambient noise in the room varied from 45 to 70 decibels. Before the ecstasy, the equipment was tested on a blind, but otherwise normal child and the graph obtained was normal.

The first graph was obtained from the tests carried out on Ivan with 70 decibels to the right ear (the auditory function of the left ear was deadened by the other ear-phone).

IVAN 29 December 1984

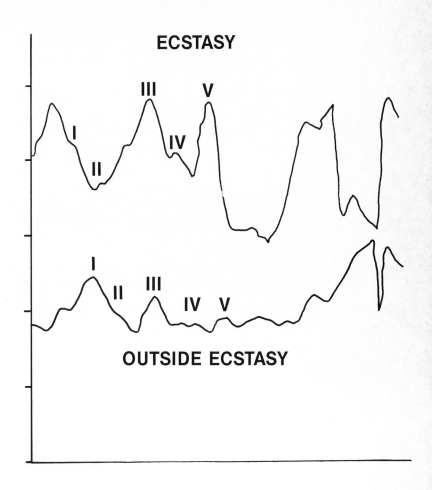

In the lower curve (before the ecstasy) 70 decibels are injected into Ivan's left ear.
In the upper curve (during the ecstasy) 90 decibels are injected.
The auditory organs function normally in both curves.
Our tests have not explored what happened afterwards. But Ivan did not react or hear anything during the ecstasy.

Technical details: alternating polarity, gain of 5, duration of 12.5ms (milliseconds) number of crossings 1,600 stimulus, 30/s.

Result: The internal I.T. I-V (time interval between waves I and V) = 4.6ms which corresponds to the normal conductivity of the auditory nerves thus indicating that the auditory pathways are organically and functionally normal as far as the relevant section of the brain. There is no tumour of the auditory nerve.

During the ecstasy: while the left ear was 'deafened' a 90 decibel sound was fed to the right ear. This is equivalent to the noise of a combustion engine at high speed. The constants remain identical to those of the preceding examination.

Result: We obtained an organised trace without modification of the interval IT: I-V = 4.6ms.

3. Results

During the ecstasy, absence of normal objective clinical reactions — in particular, when 90 decibels were fed into the right ear there was no indication of surprise. There was no subjective perception of the clicks from the right earphone while the left ear was 'deafened'. At the end of the ecstasy Ivan confirmed that he had heard nothing.

During the ecstasy, even during the recitation of the Our Father and the Gloria in the croatian language (this was heard by the others present) Ivan heard nothing.

There is, therefore, a disconnection of the auditory pathways during the ecstasy.

The auditory potentials test, which studies the nervous influx from the periphery (the cochlea, part of the inner ear) to the core of the cerebral artery, indicates that the various pathways to the brain are normal. The regular and rounded shape of the graph eliminates auditory hallucination of an epileptic type.

J Voice function (phonation)

This study was completed by Dr Francois Rouquerol during the fourth medical mission (28 December 1984).

1. Two questions were raised:

— How do the visionaries' voices disappear twice during the course of the ecstasy?

— Does the larynx function during these silent periods since gesticulation is not suppressed?

2. A physiopathological note

Every modification of the larynx function has a concomitant functioning of the muscles of the roof of the palate and thus of the internal and external peristaphyline muscles.

The action of the peristaphyline muscles modifies the intratympanic pressures and thus brings about a modification of acoustic impedance which can be recorded by an impedanceometer.

functioning of larynx muscles
↑
concomitant functioning of muscles of roof of palate
↑
action of the peristaphyline muscles
↑
modification of recordable acoustic impedance

Thus, changes in the needle in the imedpanceometer indicate variations in the larynx function; inversely, if the needle remains still, we have an indication of the immobility of the larynx.

3. Technical details
The test was administered to Ivanka on 28 December. Ambient noise, measured on a noise meter, varied between 45 and 70 decibels.

4. Results
During the prayer, recited aloud before the ecstasy, the needle (which measured the sound of the words of the visionaries) moved very widely.

As soon as the voice disappeared, at the beginning of the ecstasy, the needle stoped moving even when Vicka spoke (with very noticeable movements of the lips).

When the voices returned simultaneously to take up the Our Father (the first words of which are spoken by the Virgin) and the Gloria, the needle again moved very widely.

In the final phase, when the voices of the visionaries, apparently in conversation with the Virgin, became inaudible, the needle again became immobile. Whether they spoke — as their lip movements indicated — or not, the equipment which records phonation registered nothing. Everything took place as if the larynx function (where phonation takes place) had stopped, without any modification in the articulation of a language by the lips and the muscles that control the lips. This is yet a further argument for the exclusion of catalepsy.

IV Discussion and conclusion

A. Discussion
1. The role of the medical tests
— Our tests are by no means exhaustive. They did, however, happen and were carried out with the consent of the interested parties (and, they tell us, with the consent of the person whom they see) despite a definite reticence at the beginning.

— Not all the tests are of equal importance. The electro-encephelographs, the electro-oculographs and the evoked auditory potential tests are more important than the electrocardiograph.

No single one of them nor, indeed, any new or further tests, could offer scientific proof that the Virgin appeared to the visionaries at Medjugorje. New tests or the repetition and multiplication of those already carried out are possible, but we believe that the results we already have give us sufficient grounds for serious scientific conclusions.

2. Interpretation of the medical tests

Some might claim that certain clinical data are subjective and therefore less scientific. However, they are based on sound medical judgement and on common sense. In the last analysis it is not necessary to be a doctor in order to be aware that these young people are normal and healthy in mind, soul and body.

Paraclinical data derived from the study of the main functions and the essential organs have no aim beyond answering the question: Are there changes during the ecstasy?

3. Objective and subjective vision

This is an essential question which the tests do not answer with certainty. However, two observations would incline one towards the subjective, while three others indicate objectivity:

a. For the subjective case:

— The screening test does not impair the vision, therefore the normal visual pathways are not used.

— The evoked auditory potentials test proves that during the ecstasy the auditory pathways remain normal but are not used.

b. For the objective case:

— The convergence of their gaze as confirmed by video recording made face-on to the visionaries during the ecstasy.

— The simultaneity of the cessation of eyeball movements as established by electro-oculography.

— The simultaneous raising of their eyes and heads as the apparition disappears upwards.

If the vision is objective, and the above points would seem to indicate this, the modalities of the vision are not those of ordinary perception; they belong to another mode of perception, itself objective, but not measurable by our tests (which nevertheless do not exclude it).

B. Conclusion

Medical study, both clinical and para-clinical, of the visionaries of Medjugorje allows us to affirm that the period of ecstasy represents an extraordinary phenomenon during which, nevertheless, certain normal physiological parameters, identical to those observed before and after, are still present.

1. Identical characteristics before, during and after the ecstasy

— Electroencephalogram

— Photomotor reflexes

— Electrocardiogram

— Integrity of the auditory pathways studied in the 'evoked auditory potentials' test at least as far as the cortex or sub-cortex area.

2. Characteristics of the ecstasy at Medjugorje

These can be summarised in a number of successive points following on the functions studied.

Brain function

— Overall electrical functioning of the brain in the two visionaries studied is comparable to that of normal subjects.

— The electroencephalographic recording indicates the presence of beta rhythm interrupted by alpha, before the ecstasy. Beta rhythm corresponds to a rapid tracing of 19-20 cycles/sec. It could follow on 'an intentional effort at attention, the action of an unexpected stimulus, a strong emotion during the state of wakefulness' (*Science et Conscience*, ed. Stock, 1980, p.414). At the beginning of the ecstasy beta rhythm lasts for a short time and is replaced by almost continuous alpha rhythm. Alpha rhythm is observed in 'an attitude of expectation, during relaxation and during meditation exercises. It is a rhythm of expectation rather than attention. Attention is marked by beta'. According to Georges Pegand (*Science et Conscience*, ed. Stock, 1980, p.414), 'Contemplatives and mystics are capable of entering rapidly into alpha rhythm or of bringing about an increase in the abundance, range and regularity of alpha rhythm. It is doubtless the sign of *hesychia* (repose, quiet); it is the general state of the contemplative, the fruit of silence and thought, as described by Evagrus the Pontiac: "force yourself to keep the intellect deaf and dumb through prayer and then you will be able to pray".'

— The cerebral cortex perceives neither auditory nor visual stimulation in the surrounding environment during the ecstasy (evoked auditory potentials test and screening test).

Ocular and visual function
Significant diminution of 50 per cent for some, down to 0 per cent for others, in eyelid movement (a necessary physiological stimulus to keep the cornea moist by the application of tear secretions; the general rate is from 15/20 per minute).

— Convergence of gaze which is verified on the video recording of 28 December 1984.

— Suppression of the blinking reflex in the face of 'threat' or dazzling light.

— Simultaneity of cessation of eyeball movement at the beginning of the ecstasy (to the nearest one-fifth of a second) (oculographic recording of Ivan and Marija) and simultaneous recommencement of movement (again to the nearest one-fifth of a second) at the end of the ecstasy.

Cardiac function
Slight changes in heart rate: slower for Marija and Ivanka and slightly accelerated in the cases of Ivan and Vicka.

— Slight change in blood pressure, tending to become lower (Ivanka, Ivan).

— Normal cardiac contractions (electrocardiogram).

Voice function
Cessation of larynx function during the two silent periods of the ecstasy without modification of the muscles controlling gesticulation.

Auditory function
Inhibition of the auditory function which is demonstrated by the fact that Ivan claims not to hear when 90 decibels are applied to his right ear; though he has received no warning, he does not jump when the sound is fed into his ear.

Experts' conclusions

The phenomenon of the apparition in Medjugorje, which was studied during five different periods of 1984 with five visionaries as subjects, is scientifically inexplicable. Clinical observation of the visionaries leads us to affirm, as our Yugoslav colleagues have already affirmed, that these young people are healthy in mind and body.

Detailed clinical and paraclinical studies completed before, during and after the ecstasies of 24-25 March, 9-10 June, 6-7 October and 28-29 December allow us to affirm scientifically that there is no pathological modification of the parameters studied: electro-encephalogram, electrocardiogram, evoked auditory potentials.

— There is no epilepsy, as electro-encephalograms demonstrate.

- They are not asleep; again the electro-encephalograms demonstrate this.
- There is no question of hallucination in the pathological sense of that word:

- There is no auditory or visual hallucination that would be linked to the peripheral auditory or visual receptors (normal visual and auditory pathways).

- There is no paroxystic hallucination: the electro-encephalograms demonstrate this.

- There are no hallucinations that would have their origins in dream such as one would observe in cases of extreme mental disorder or in the course of the development of atrophic dementia.

- There is no question of catalepsy, because, during the ecstasy the muscles controlling gesticulation are not inhibited and function normally.

The eyeball movements stop and restart simultaneously (to the second). During the ecstasy there is a face-to-face meeting, as it were, between the visionaries and a person whom we did not see. The young people's behaviour is always non-pathological; during the ecstasy they are in a 'state of prayer' and interpersonal communication. The visionaries of Medjugorje are not drop-outs or dreamers, nor are they tired or anxious; they are free and happy, at home in their country and in the modern world.

The ecstasies are not pathological nor is there any element of deceit. No scientific discipline seems able to describe these phenomena. We would be quite willing to define them as a state of active, intense prayer, partially disconnected from the outside world, a state of contemplation with a separate person whom they alone can see, hear and touch.

Dr Frigerio's tests, 8-10 March 1985
The situation on Thursday 8 March

Dr Frigerio, who arrived on Thursday 8 March with two colleagues (an ear, nose and throat specialist and an ophthalmologist) did not do any test on the first day. Members of the episcopal commission had been present on the previous day (Wednesday). They were present at the ecstasy and kept repeating ironically 'Ode, Ode' (she is gone) and when they questioned the visionaries it was in the following vein:

> 'What message from the Virgin did Tomislav Vlasic tell you to reveal today?' (They believed that Father Tomislav invented the messages.)

The interrogation was painful. Ivan had some difficulty with the secret sign, having gone too far. They needed to regroup in prayer, particularly since a friend of theirs, a young Croatian Franciscan, had died.

Vicka, Friday 8 March

On that same Friday evening Vicka awaited an apparition at about 21.30 with a message. (Her health and the wishes of the apparition had delayed her.) The doctors arrived and with her permission attached a laryngophone to her larynx (this equipment is used on patients who have undergone laryngectomy; it picks up what is said at a level below that which is externally audible). But the apparition ended very quickly, after twenty-two seconds. The apparatus functioned for an instant but not long enough to allow any interpretation, and then it stopped. The ecstasy had ceased.

Vicka explained. The Virgin greeted me saying, 'May God be praised', and I answered, 'May he be praised.' It was at that moment that the apparatus functioned. But then the Virgin said, looking at the apparatus, '*Is is not necessary*'. Then she left smiling. She did not show annoyance. But the expected message was not given to Vicka until the subsequent apparition (on the following day, if I understand correctly).

Tests on Saturday

On Saturday the doctor attached a stapedium to Ivan; this instrument explores the functioning of the inner ear. When Ivan knelt down the instrument fell out of his ear and thus the test failed. An ocular test was, however, completed; it examined the eyelid reflexes and obtained the same results as our tests.

2
Fasting

Medjugorje has helped to revive the practice of fasting. This movement is helping to spread and sharpen the spontaneous rediscovery of fasting which, after a long decline, is now happening: fasting is dead, long live fasting! This renewal is proceeding along the same lines as those recommended by John Paul II, who saw fit to retain this tradition in Canon Law even though many had thought it to be outmoded.

Hundreds of thousands[1] now practise fasting on bread and water following the invitation of Our Lady at Medjugorje — and are feeling all the better for it, body and soul. What is the meaning of this? How are we to avoid the pitfalls and the counter-indications of fasting? How are we to practise fasting fruitfully following the furrow ploughed by Jesus and the Gospel? It may be well to reintroduce into Christian history and tradition this phenomenon of the Medjugorje fast in order to answer these questions on a spiritual and medical level.

Origins
Since the Medjugorje fast is now a living movement, a fact of life, people will want to know precisely how fasting was revived by the apparitions. It is more complex than would appear at first sight.

Jozo Zovko's meeting
During the second week of the apparitions, at the beginning of July, (perhaps the 2nd) the Parish priest, Jozo, was in the church in the early afternoon. He was still perplexed about the apparitions, of which there was so much talk, and during his prayer he heard an inner voice saying to him: — 'Go outside the church and protect the children.'

The visionaries were at that moment being followed by the police. They were fleeing across the fields, running towards the church. They appeared just at the moment Jozo left the church. They were very upset, and some

---

1. I have been able to check this fact during the course of my journeys in Italy, France and even in the US, where communities of sometimes more than a thousand people are fasting once a week.

of them were crying. The parish priest took them into the presbytery and the apparition took place. He called the parishioners together for a Mass at 5.00. Crowds of local people arrived and in this difficult situation he invited them to take a stance before God.

'Are you ready to pray and fast (for three days)?'
The answer was firm and enthusiastic:
'Yes, that is what we want.'

The tradition of Hercegovina
It began as an initiative on the part of the parish priest; there was not as yet a message from the Virgin. How did he get this idea? Perhaps it was inspiration but above all he was basing himself on an ancient tradition of Bosnia-Hercegovina. Ever since the period of the persecution, which inspired so much heroism, fasting was an honoured practice both in times of difficulty and on the vigils of important feasts.

A twelve-day fast was observed before the feast of the Assumption and for certain other feasts. This was called 'eating dry'. It was a bread and water fast but certain additions, notably fruit, were allowed. In fact, the fast of Saint Roch called for fruit only.

These fasts had been discarded and were practised only by a few elderly and apparently old-fashioned ladies. Before anything was said at the apparitions, the very fact that they took place and the serious situation which they created in an officially atheistic country, reawakened and enlivened this dying tradition, giving it a new meaning and a new aim: count on God, open youself to his coming through concrete privation, thus cultivating your faculties of prayer, intercession and conversion.

Biblical tradition
The tradition of the people of Hercegovina was rooted in biblical revelation. Fasting (Hebrew: *zom*, Greek: *nesteria*, Latin: *jejunium*) appears frequently in the Old Testament. According to the Book of Ezra it was abstention from food from morning to sunset (*Ez 10:31*). Fasts for two or three days were recommended (*Est 4:10*) or even sometimes for a whole week. Tradition attributes to Moses (*Ex 24:18; 34:28*), Elijah (*1 K 19:8*) and Jesus (*Lk 4:2*) a fast for forty days and forty nights and, in the case of Moses, excluded both food and drink.

The fast is a time for prayer and encounter with God (*Ex 34:28*), for Sabbath repose (*Lk 16:29.31; 23,32*), a time for openness to God. Moses (*Ex 34,28*) and Daniel (*Dn 9:3; 10:2-8*) fasted for a long period before receiving divine revelation.

Fasts are a penitent expression of conversion (*Nbs 28,29; Jr 14:12* cf. *Jdg 20:26*; *Jon 3:5-10*). They anticipate (*Jl 2:12-17*; *Jon 3:5-10*), avert(*1 Sam 7;6*), or follow on a disaster or chastisement *Jdg 20;26*).

The law prescribed a fast only for the feast of expiation: a day of rest and common prayer (*Lv 16:29-31; 23:27-32, Nbs 29:7*) to which was added after the exile a day of fasting in remembrance of the destruction of Jerusalem (*Zac 7:3*). Fasting is sometimes associated with mourning (*1 Mc 3:46-48*). The inhabitants of Jabesh-Gilead fasted after burying Saul and his sons (*Is 31:13*), similarly David after the death of Jonathan:

> Then David took hold of his clothes and rent them; and so did all the men who were with him; and they mourned and wept and fasted until evening for Saul and for Jonathan his son and for the people of the Lord and for the house of Israel, because they had fallen by the sword. (*2 Sm 1:11*)

Nevertheless, David changed this usage after the death of his infant son born to him of his adulterous relationship with Uriah's wife. He fasted as long as the child lived and had a repast served when he died. This underlines one of the principal functions of fasts: intercession. Some seemed surprised and David said:

> While the child was still alive, I fasted and wept for I said, 'who knows whether the Lord will be gracious to me that the child may live?' But now he is dead, why should I fast? Can I bring him back again? I shall go to him, but he will not return to me. (*2 Sam 12, 22-23*).

This function of intercession in serious situations is illustrated in many texts (*Jg 20:26; 1 Sm 7:6; Jl. 2:12,17*) where fasting goes hand in hand with prophetic preaching, inviting repentance and admission of sins.

Recourse was made to fasts against plagues and threats (*Est 4:3; 9:31; 2 Ch 20:3*). Ezra and his companions undertook a fast in support of their project to return (*Ez 8; 21, 23*) and they then did penance when they discovered that they had sinned by marrying foreign women (*Ne 9:1*).

Fasting to atone for sin had nothing to do with superstition. According to Sirach one must fast to atone for sin but by sinning again one destroys the effect (*Si 34:26*). People fasted in order to implore God's pardon (*1 K 21:27*) or to attune themselves to the light of God (*Dn 10:12*).

Fasts cultivated openness to God, but, we are tempted to add, one must also share in the poverty of God. According to the Gospel the poor are 'blessed' (*Mt 5:1*) and filled with the happiness of God, and God recognises himself more in the poor than in the rich. Why? The rich accumulate possessions and the poor are reduced to existing. In a transcendent sense God also is existence. His creatures are not possessions for his aggrandisement. He made them free, capable of loving him but capable also of revolting against him. He invites us not to count on possessions but on existence, not on accumulation but on silence: another sign from God. Fasting from food facilitates interior fasting. It is not a question of possessing God as a possession but rather of existing with him, by him and like him in the depths of peace and silence.

The gospel

In the New Testament John the Baptist lives with his disciples in the desert on locusts and wild honey. (*Mt 3:4;11:18* & *Mk 2:18*). The practice is totally associated with the conversion and baptism which he preaches.

Jesus himself, in preparation for his ministry, fasts in the desert as a sign of total abandonment to the Father (*Mt 4:1-4*; Lk 4:1-4). On the fortieth day he was hungry with that deep hunger which is the organism's final warning before death. He does not use his power to save his life: 'Man shall not live by bread alone but by every word that proceeds from the mouth of God' (*Mt 4:4-5*; *Lk 4:1-4*) Jesus answers, quoting from Deuteronomy.

Nevertheless, neither he nor his disciples seem to have fasted on the prescribed days (*Ac 27:9*) for Jesus wished to distance himself from the ageing practices made sterile by that formalism which is condemned in the parable where the Pharisee 'fasts twice a week'. This is perfectly in keeping with the prophetic tradition.

While distancing himself from the traditional practices Jesus is also quiteliberal about dining 'at the table of the publicans and sinners' (*Mk 2:16*; *Mt 9:11*; *Lk 5:30*) whom he invites into the Kingdom. The festive meal offered by Matthew to celebrate his conversion gives expression to the Gospel message. There is more joy in heaven over one sinner who is converted than over the ninety-nine who did not need conversion. Fasting is not a rigourist practice; it is not self-affliction or self-destruction; it is not a permanent state. Far from forbidding festive meals, Jesus is in favour of them and spiritualises them: food becomes a sign of sharing. It leads to the heavenly banquet: super-substantial food. He prepares for this spiritual banquet by material abstention.

Fasting does not mean despising food, or material goods or hospitality. Jesus insists on the point: his disciples should not fast while the bridegroom is with them (*Mk 2:19*; *Mt 9:14,17*; Lk 5:35-39).

In spite of this frugality while journeying — he rubbed the ears of corn in his hands (*Mk 2:23* and parables) — the refreshing attitude of Jesus prepares the way for a different type of fast, less juridical, more inspirational, more oriented towards the fullness of the heavenly banquet.

> I tell you many will come from the east and west and sit at the table of Abraham, Isaac and Jacob in the kingdom of heaven. (*Mt 8:11*)

When the bridegroom has been taken away (*Mk 2:20*) fasting will again find a place. Jesus seems to have alluded to this on the occasion of a particularly difficult exorcism. This kind of demon cannot be cast out except by prayer and fasting — but the word 'fasting' is missing in the best translations (*Mk 9:29* and all the verses of *Mt 17:21*).

In the early communities

Fasting prepared the early charismatic communities for the motions of the Spirit and prepared Paul's and Barnabas' first mission to the pagan world. (*Acts 13:3*) Prayer and fasting were associated with the installation of presbyters in the communities established by Paul and Barnabas (*Acts 14:23*). The mention of the legal fast for the feast of Expiation (*Acts 27:9*) leads us to believe that the Apostle had retained this practice. In the second letter to the Corinthians he twice mentions his many fasts (*2 Co 6:5* and *11:27*) in spite of his many tribulations. Fasting ought to be understood in its broadest sense; ritual and spiritual. The word refers to Paul's entire ascetic way of life.

Biblical meaning of fasting

Fasting (Hebrew *zom*) is characterised by the expression, *anah nephes*, which means poverty in spirit. The word *anah* is the root meaning of the poor, the humble, the little people: '*anawim*'. To fast is to recognise one's poverty, one's humility before God, (joyfully and freely) cultivating the soil for God's seed. Thus the words *anah nephes*, which originally had a broad meaning, came to be a specific designation of fasting in Leviticus (*Lv 16; 29-31;23;27-32; Nb 29:7; Dn 10:2*). To fast is to humble oneself (*Lv 16:29*). It means the recognition of one's dependence on God and the opening of one's heart to him alone. It means giving up the goods of this world in order to find that hundredfold (*Mk 10:20*) which God alone, through our detachment, can give. This is said with great clarity in Deuteronomy:

> (and you shall remember all the ways which the Lord God has led you)… And he humbled you and let you hunger and fed you with manna, which you did not know, nor did your fathers know; that he might make you know that man does not live by bread alone, but that man lives by everything that proceeds out of the mouth of the Lord. (*Dt 8:3-5*)

This saying is reaffirmed by Jesus at the end of his fast (*Mt 4:4; Lk 4:4*). Apart from the negative dimension of humility, fasting also involves a divine dimension of plenty.

There is also a community aspect. The fasts of the Old Testament are very often 'publicly convened' (*Jr 36:9; 2 Ch 20:3; Er 8:21* etc). Such fasts, through collective solidarity, gave public and tangible expression to a relationship with God; sackcloth and ashes (*Ne 9:1; Est 4:1-3; Dn 9:3; Jon 3,5; Mt 11:21; Lk 10:13* etc).

As would later be the case with Jesus, the prophets scarcely speak of fasting. Zechariah only mentions fasts that commemorate the fall of Jerusalem (*Zc 7:3; 3:5; 8:19*) in order to underline the future days of joy, rejoicing and happiness (*8:19*). The prophets do not speak of legal fasts. Why? Because of their reaction to formalism. When they do speak of them it is to condemn their empty ritualism and to give them a new meaning, oriented towards justice (*Is 58; 2; Jr 14,12; Zc 7:5-14;* see *Ps 51*). They spiritualised it, revitalised it, saw it as a stage int he journey towards the heavenly feast. This is the thinking that was fulfilled in Jesus Christ.

History
Early enthusiasm
Fasting (like celibacy for the sake of the Kingdom) takes on the meaning of an eschatological challenge, the renunciation of everything — even the better and most necessary things of life — in order to count on God alone. The Didache recommends: Fasting for those who persecute you (*1;3*). The candidate for baptism should fast for one or two days before being baptised (*7;4*). This very quickly becomes a common practice (Justin, 2nd century, *Apologia 1,61* and Hippolytus, *Apostolic Traditio, 20*). This fast was a sharing in Christ's death and would lead to his resurrection.

The Fathers of the desert pushed this challenge to its limits, to the point of ostentation in the case of the stylites, perched on top of their high columns. People were perhaps too impressed by the performance though in fact this phenomenon did have some success. It was easy to forget that all this was the outcome of an experience of prayer and total self-giving to God.

But, for the Christian community, in Rome and elsewhere fasting was oriented, in moderation, towards charity. St Leo (died 461) saw two aspects to fasting: personal and communal.

> Each one should in his diet take account of those that are hungry. (*Sermons 11:1*)

> The abstinence of the person who fasts should become the food of the poor man. (*Sermons 13:1*)

> What each one removes from his own satisfaction should be consecrated to the poor and the miserable. (*Sermons 4:6*)

He underlines the benefits of fasting:

> Health in freedom and freedom in health, the body being ruled by the mind and the mind by the help of God. (*Sermons 1;2*)

Fasting helps to conquer the devil, to overcome the passions; it gives rise 'to pure thoughts, reasonable desires and salutary counsels'. (*Sermons 13:1*) But St Leo is less insistent on this aspect of 'inner hygiene' than on openness to God and to others. This experience of poverty helps us to understand the poor.

Let each one recognise in himself his condition of changeable, perishable mortality and, because of this common condition, let him treat his neighbour with fraternal love. (*Sermons 11:1*)

The discipline of fasting
The Church wisely included the benefits of fasting in the institutions of Christian life: the Vigils, Quartertense (three days of fasting at the beginning of each season, fifth century) and, above all, since the fourth century, Lent, the long fast of forty days in imitation of the Lord who was himself repeating the experiences of Moses and Elijah on the journey to Horeb.

However, this pedagogy of humility and moderation was all too frequently misunderstood as privation, abstention and self-inflicted punishment in the face of a God who was seen as morbid and even tyrannical. What a strange caricature of fasting and, indeed, of God himself! What had been discovered and understood with enthusiastic fervour was now being practised in sadness. Those who fasted thought only of being hungry, sometimes to the point of obsession, which resulted in an apathy diametrically opposed to the original Christian inspiration.

The Church, mindful of the situation, mitigated the regulations; individuals found loopholes that were now seen as extrinsic and juridical. Permission was given to add two snacks to the principal meal — for a long time the only one allowed. The morning snack allowed for 50 grammes of bread and a sweetened beverage. Liquid, it was said, did not break the fast. '*Liquid*, what might this mean?' the legal experts asked, and the common answer was 'that a substance was liquid as long as the spoon cannot stand up in it'.

Decline
In spite of these concessions, those who fasted still seemed to feel the pangs of hunger constantly. Some seminarians will remember that the Rector's humour was positively foul during Lent. I can remember them saying this at the time.

The fear of being hungry led many to stuff themselves during the main meal. They simply ate too much. A monastery cook told me that greater quantities of food were consumed during Lent than over a comparable period during the rest of the year. The balance sheet was there to prove it. The one unrestricted meal simply became excessive. To the sense of privation were added the ill-effects of over-eating, dilation of the stomach and digesetive problems. This was the very contradiction of fasting. Father Rouillard writes in *Catholicisme* 6 (1967, col. 833):

> Nowadays people no longer fast. Today, fasting appears anachronistic and impractical... if perchance we try, we get the impression that fasting brings about a state that is the exact opposite of that described

in the preface for Lent: 'curbing of vice, elevation of the soul, giving of strength'. Today fasting is one of those observances that have been abandoned.

Was the quasi-disappearance of this degraded form of fasting necessary for the rediscovery of the practice of fasting?

Secular rediscovery

In our society, where illness is more often due to excess than to privation and where inequalities between rich and poor are growing to scandalously serious proportions, fasting has been rediscovered in many quarters over the past few years.

We now have specialists in obesity. Doctors regularly prescribe diets to counteract obesity and other effects of over-eating. Of course patients do not always play the game, exceptions are created and sneak visits are made to the fridge. But at least in principle, frugality is accepted. A number of business people, patrons of costly restaurants, are now 'giving a miss' to the midday meal. The 'big feed' is no longer fashionable. It is now somewhat shameful and is despised.

Abuses of alcohol and tobacco have provoked spontaneous reactions well beyond the confines of Christianity. Non-smoking areas are extended in planes, trains and taxis. The French hierarchy, Lourdes meeting, October 1984, after long hesitation has finally recommended abstention from tobacco and alcohol, without laying down any regulations.

Ecological groups, those advocating a return to nature (Shelton) underline the importance of fasting in one's life.

Fasting as a sign of protest has become part of the news. In Ireland, the hunger strikers who fasted to death held the world in suspense. Those young protestors, who somehow command our respect, are not without their counterparts in the spiritual order. Their gesture is spectacular and absolute and leads easily to a blind radicalism against which we must be on our guard even if we admire the heroism of those who go to these extremes. Christian fasting is moderate, modest and constructive.

The rediscovery of fasting is natural and secular. But there is also a Christian rediscovery.

Christian rediscovery

In some schools in France and Germany and elsewhere the custom of fasting on a bowl of rice on certain days during Lent, is now gaining ground. Rice is simple food and it is economical; moreover it is the staple food of the starving millions in Asia. The difference in cost is donated to feeding the hungry. As a result, large sums of money are sent annually to underdeveloped countries. This is perfectly in line with one of the biblical dimensions of fasting: justice and solidarity according to the prophets.

Fasting is widespread in the charasmatic renewal movement.

The 'Mère de Miséricorde'[2] movement, under the patronage of the Virgin Mary, established groups in 1984 that fasted for periods of ten days. Ten persons fast for ten days, each one of them for one day. The fast is strictly one of bread and water. When one of the members of the group hears of a young girl who is pregnant he or she passes on the other members her Christian name, age and the number of days remaining before she finally decides whether to keep her child or not within the framework of the help offered by the movement.

If after a period of inner struggle — sometimes lasting for days or weeks — the young woman opts for abortion, then the entire group fasts on the same day in a spirit of repentance and reparation.

If the life of the child is saved, then the ten members of the group share a eucharistic celebration in a spirit of thanksgiving for this victory for mercy.

The practice of fasting at Medjugorje belongs to this tradition:

- It is not a radical fast, self-exalting or self-scrutinising but provokes openness to God and to others;
- It is not a performance but is humble and modest;
- It is not morbid self-affliction but the sign of a joyful return to God.

These movements came before the deliberate restoration decided on by John Paul II. Canon law reform, in the first instance, took cognisance of the decline, amounting to disappearance, that was taking place in many countries. The Pope insisted on retaining traditional Friday abstinence as well as the practice of fasting on Ash Wednesday and Good Friday (Canon 1251).

The message of Medjugorje

Revelation, the tradition of Hercegovina, modern insights, and the critical situation on 2 July 1981, all conbined to inspire Father Jozo Zovko to take the initiative out of which the Medjugorje fast was born.

Father Tomislav questioned the visionaries about this message on 21 July 1983. He noted the responses given by Our Lady:

1. The best fast is that of bread and water.

2. Fasting can avert wars.

3. It can cause natural laws to be suspended.

These latter two surprising statements remind us of the gospel sayings on faith 'capable of moving mountains' (*Mt 17:20*) and on the demons who

---

2. Mère de Miséricorde (Mother of Mercy), Couvent Notre Dame, 81170 Cordes, Tel. (63) 561292.

resisted (exorcism) who can only be driven out 'by prayer and fasting' (*Mk 9:29*).

4. Almsgiving cannot replace fasting (but it can be associated with it).

5. Only for reasons of age or health are people permitted to substitute prayer, almsgiving and confession for fasting. Everyone must fast except the ill.

Helena, whose messages had a pedagogical effect on the parish, adds: 'There are different ways of fasting: we should fast on bread and water but we should also abstain from television. It is a network that makes prayer impossible'. This is an invitation to us to discover what it is that clutters our lives and our minds, making us incapable of openness to God, silence, prayer and conversion. Fasting on bread and water is a basic corporal technique which stimulates openness to the essential.

Good practice

The spirit

How are we to fast? According to the biblical meaning, it involves poverty, privation, humility and thus restriction. Fasting means eating less than we would spontaneously. Though the invitation from Our Lady to fast on bread and water lays down no guidelines as to the quantity, each person should discover the level of reduction that suits their make-up, temperament and life-style without reducing them to anxiety or narrowmindedness.

The body

Fasting does not mean going hungry. In the early stages this impression arises. It can have the power of a fixation, an obsession. But this is not real hunger (a much more radical sensation that is rarely if ever experienced by the peoples of Europe). It is perhaps an appetite that is exacerbated by our fixation, a simple nervous tension, an anxiety feeling. We can forget it simply by concentrating on something else. These are the twinges felt by the long distance traveller on arrival in a foreign country even though he may have eaten on the plane. Or again it may resemble the feelings of emptiness felt by the scholar on ending a long night's intellectual work. These mini-sensations, which can sometimes cause dizziness or giddiness, have no functional significance. During a fast undertaken in the proper Christian spirit they are readily forgotten by thinking about God and by facing our daily tasks in his company.

Fasting represents an apprenticeship. We grow into it. In the beginning there will be hunger spasms. These are overcome not through repression or voluntary acts of self-control but rather by changing this material hunger into spiritual hunger for God.

Fasting does not mean weakening oneself, unsettling oneself. It is liberating. It ought, therefore, to be undertaken in a measured and orderly fashion. It is up to each one to find the right measure.

Fasting does not lead to a diminished life of inactivity. It does not suppress, does not weaken as much as we might be led to believe. The diminished supply of energy helps to tone up the Christian, spiritually and mentally. Frequently, on a day after fasting — provided we avoid compensatory over-indulgence — we feel much more invigorated.

Even a more radical fast[3] on bread and water does not diminish our strength as much as we might think. We can still carry on our normal intellectual or even physical work, provided the fast does not go on for too long. This is the secret of a healthy economy. Some people made this discovery in the tragic famines of long ago. Those were the ones who best learned how to survive. But we should be careful not to become undernourished; this would represent a deviation from the true meaning of fasting which should allow us to give of our best, even healthwise.

We would be ill-advised to fast on very busy, overcrowded days. When one fasts it is better to ease the pace slightly, cut out the bustle,try to achieve peace and calm. Feverish activity would neutralise or at least put at risk the beneficial effects of fasting. Undertaken in this spirit fasting will help to relax the nerves, ease the tensions.

It increases the demand for sleep, a demand that is better heeded than denied. In fact, one of the benefits of fasting may well lie in remedying insomnia.

Fasting then is not inactivity; it blends well with the biblical idea of Sabbath repose, very appropriate in time of retreat.

Do not fast on Sundays

Without doubt the calm that we can sometimes enjoy on a Sunday creates the proper conditions for fasting and it should not be excluded for someone who can manage the luxury of a lonely retreat on that day. But Sunday is the day of the Lord: 'can the friends of the Bridegroom be in mourning while the Bridegroom is with them?'

Sunday is a feastday, a day when we might model ourselves on Jesus at Cana, or at the table of Matthew the publican or of other sinners. We should celebrate socially, in the family or in the community. In these celebrations the body and the food have an important role (without excess or dietary abberation!). Fasting despises neither the food nor the dining table. It should on the contrary lead us to a better understanding of both as gifts of God. God's 'hundredfold' is not quantity, it is the quality which one finds in healthy moderation and in acts of thanksgiving.

Counter-indications

If one is not well-prepared psychologically and spiritually it is better not

---

3. Radical fasting can be undertaken occasionally: Ash Wednesday or Good Friday. The words of Lanza del Vasto are apt: 'For today, Lord, you will be my only bread'.

to fast. It would be preferable to go through a period of calm preparation than to throw oneself in at the deep end. We do not fast with a view to putting ourselves out of step but rather to build up our strengths, making us healthier, more vigorous, better equipped for the service of the Lord. Once again, a tense lifestyle and feverish activity will not be conducive to fasting. There may well be counter-indications from a medical point of view (see the medical note by Professor Henri Joyeux on p. 96).

Essentials

The foregoing 'ecological' considerations are mere accessories; let us return to the essentials. The fast requested by Our Lady at Medjugorje is of a modest, non-radical nature. It avoids the dangers of light-headedness and of being turned in on oneself; it avoids undernourishment. This is the meaning of the advice: 'the best fast is on bread and water'. Let nobody undertake a fast unless in a spirit of joy, calmness, openness to God and to others; let privation be understood as fulfilling for it leads to the hundredfold promised in the Gospel: more careful use and a better understanding of the goods of this world. This is so, for by fasting our passions give way to self-control; greedy possession gives way to freedom, the sadness of the rich young man to the joy of Francis of Assisi.

This is the spirit of the fast on bread and water recommended by Our Lady of Medjugorje.

— The bread should, if possible, be wholemeal. This is much healthier and makes up for the deficiencies of white flour. It is a pity that the wholesome bread of long ago should be more expensive than white bread and has almost become a luxury.

— Plenty of water should be taken. Normally one and a half to two litres will be necessary.

— Some fruit is permissible for those who find that bread alone is not suitable.

The mother of a family undertook a fast but soon found that she was suffering from a headache. Her husband, a doctor, diagnosed hypoglycaemia (lack of sugar). She wisely stopped fasting, not wishing to impose the consequences on her children. On her next attempt, she added some fruit. This is the most natural remedy for hypoglycaemia and, at the same time, it diminishes the risk of the constipation experienced by some. Fruit, being a natural food, is better than sugar which is concentrated and artificial and may in any case have the opposite effect (exhaustion and drowsiness) to that desired.

As we have already said, fruit has its place in the old tradition of fasting; it supplies a liquid element thus permitting a small reduction in the quantity of water indicated above. Concessions to human weakness are part and parcel of the humility which characterises fasting, according to the Bible.

Fasting does not consist of stuffing oneself with bread or of eating haphazardly here and there. We should eat in a more restrained and moderate fashion at the normal hours: two or three pieces of bread are normally sufficient to supply enough energy for our daily activity; any further energies needed are taken by the organism from our reserves which are often excessive (to a greater or lesser degree according to each individual).

Let us recapitulate the beneficial effects of fasting:

— Negatively: it eliminates toxins which are destroyed by the undernourished body (this happens all the more so in the case of a radical fast of water only which can be tried on Ash Wednesday or Good Friday). Bodily purification is a sign of, and an aid to purification of the mind which attains God through humility. The body and the mind are more closely associated than one would think.

— Positively: fasting gives us supremacy over our basic desires and supremacy of the mind over the body. It teaches us to stand back from our impulses and from the goods of the world. It does not repress them but keeps them in order. It opens us to our neighbour in a spirit of compassion and mutual help. It opens us to God himself.

Fasting is a small and humble means of freeing the mind by orienting the body towards God. The state of the body is an intimate and fundamental indication of the life of the spirit. Material privation, freely undertaken and properly assumed, aids us in the discovery of that chronic privation of God which we would otherwise forget. It makes us conscious of this. It stimulates this profound and primordial desire. It mobilises the resources of body and mind in order to encounter God in prayer and in charity.

Fasting is, therefore, a means among others that helps us to channel and orient our dispersed energies. This is one of the secrets of fasting: a modest but efficacious springboard to God and through him to others.

The range of fasting

Sexuality

Fasting from food is only one form among many others. It is a particularly significant form because eating, taking nourishment, is the first action of which we are capable, the most necessary for existence and for the development of the body. It is a pressing, daily need which can become disorderly or obsessional. It is important that this need be just as responsibly assumed and mastered as the sexual need which, though different and less indispensable, is related. The practice of fasting, when properly understood, has always been an aid in mastering sexuality; it is to be recommended to those who have vowed to renounce sexuality for the sake of God alone, or indeed those who are deprived of the normal exercise of sexuality through bereavement, illness, travel etc.[4] These vital instincts are essential for the conservation of personal life and the life of the species. These drives and impulses have a functional role and meaning but they are frequently violent, incoherent and disorderly. They represent passion and not freedom. Bad dietary practice ('the big feed') and excesses of sexuality (shameless or perverse eroticism) are legion. They often destroy the body, the mind, and even society itself. It is of absolute importance that these two vital instincts be responsibly assumed according to one's state in life: marriage or celibacy. Neither one of them works well without good order and discipline. Too many people are the victims of the violent disorder of their instincts. It is the cause of bodily and spiritual disorientation. Order must be restored. Popular freudianism, frequently over-simplified to the point of destruction, has spread slogans which have falsified the normal order in this area of instinct disturbed by sin.

It is too easily said and too readily accepted that to resist wild temptation is to risk repression; elemental desires are the ultimate law; the best way to deal with temptations is to yield to them; sexuality is an unconditional right which can be used arbitrarily according to one's whims, even perversions, and all of this is of no importance provided one has charity. According to this principle Marc Oraison was said to advise wayward penitents not to change their lives but to use the same charity in dealing with their wife as with their mistress. There lies the 'real moral problem' (*La Prostitution,* 1979, p.76). What a despicable attempt to manage the disorders of the passions! The tidal wave of false theories has contributed to the undermining of faith and morals. Fasting may well be one of roads leading back to a proper order, to spiritual renewal and to God himself.

The twin appetites, for sex and food, can be more readily controlled than our unbalanced erotic society would lead us to believe. For both, we ought to know how to put forgetfulness before obsession, the fullness of God before the giddy heights of the void.

Tobacco and alcohol

What has been said about the fundamental instincts for food and sex could equally be applied to other desires: tobacco and alcohol in particular. Both products are poisonous to the body.

---

4. We have to be careful because long periods of radical fasting do not favour chastity. 'The poor bed is fertile' remarked J. de Castro who studied the problems of hunger in the world. Sexual drives increase in an organism that is threatened by death. Hunger 'which makes fertile the bed of the poor', gave rise, among the fathers of the desert — who were given to extreme fasting — to the famous 'temptations of Saint Anthony' which have become proverbial. And the hermits of antiquity — the inordinate nature of their austerity has often been exaggerated — understood that apart from rare exceptions of this nature (popularised in the iconography) heaven should not be tempted. They moderated their fasts and generally adopted the fast of bread and water which Our Lady of Medjugorje recommends and is causing to be reborn in the Church.

First electro-encephalogram carried out on Ivan and Marija on Pentecost Sunday, 10 June 1984. The apparatus attached to Marija had been damaged en route and the smudged graph was illegible. Ivan's perfect graph indicates wakeful contemplative rhythm.

Before the ecstasy on 6 October, Professor Joyeux is assisted by Mr Dubois-Chabert in attaching the eight electrodes for the electro-encephalogram to Marija. In order to avoid interference the public was excluded, with the exception of a little blind Italian girl who had become friendly with Marija.

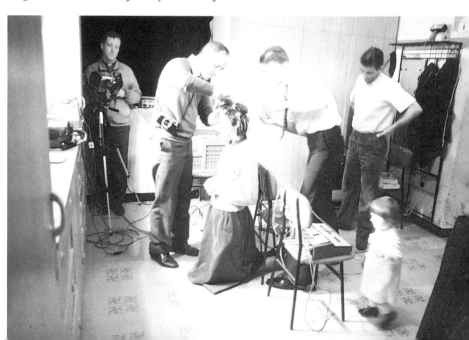

Above: The ecstasy of 6 October in the sacristy of the parish church.
Below: Before the apparition Vicka and Marija (who had just received her diploma as a hairstylist) retain their sense of humour in spite of the barrage of equipment.

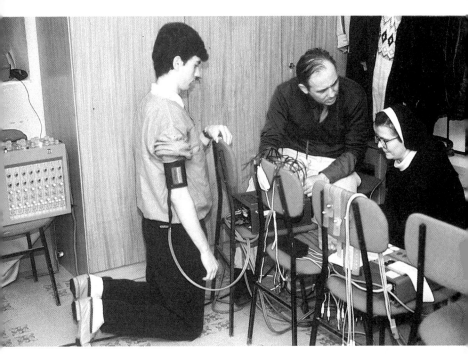

Before the ecstasy of 7 October 1984, Professor Joyeux attaches apparatus for measuring heart rhythm and blood pressure.

During the ecstasy of Sunday 7 October, Dr Philippot does a screening test on Ivanka who is wired for an electro-encephalogram. She shows no reaction to this test which did not disturb her vision.

Tests on 28 December 1984: Preparations for simultaneous electro-oculogram of Ivan and Marija have just been completed.
Bottom: electro-encephalogram of Ivanka on 7 October and Marija's screening test.

Professor Henri Joyeux attaches no scientific importance to the documents reproduced on this page. They are reproduced simply to reflect Fr Laurentin's wish to present as wide a sample as possible of the documents that are circulating among the pilgrims at Medjugorje. We cannot underline too much the restrained nature of his remarks.

Mr Colla, a professional photographer, was surprised by this image of the Cross on the breast of the statue of Our Lady of Medjugorje. The pictures (photos 1 and 2) were taken with a flash on 28 December 1984 in the parish church. Perhaps the image is explained by the reflections that are noticeable on many photos (photo 3). The photographer does not think so because he discovered the same image (paler) on another photo (4) which was taken on the dame day but with totally different lighting which should have given a totally different effect. R.L.

The luminous phenomena of Medjugorje are problematic. There has been no scientific study and they are subject to discussion. These photos are merely meant to state the question which would have been studied by an inter-disciplinary team.

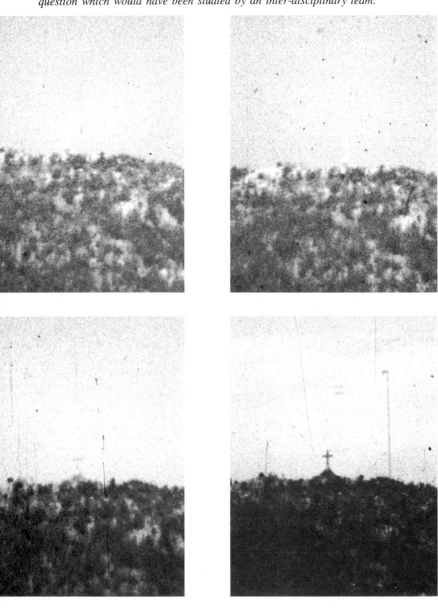

Frames from a film taken at Medjugorje by Louis Desrippes, a biologist from Bordeaux, 7 August 1984. The photograph of the film (Super 8) does not clearly show the flashing silhouette above the globe although it is quite visible on the original film. The photo is reproduced here merely as an example in the hope that qualified specialists will undertake a study of the original Super 8 film. R.L.

1. *Those who took the photo above were struck by it because the beams of light fell on the chapel while the apparitions were happening on 4 August 1984.*
2. *Cruciform rays were photographed on 8 September 1984. A keen photographer from Medjugorje claims that this is totally explicable through the refractions caused by an open diaphragm and a wide angle lens.*

On 14 September 1983, a woman from Mostar who had photographed the crowd in prayer was surprised to find this silhouette of the Virgin and the cross on the photo. She was not photographing in the direction of Krizevac. Renzo Rivoli took this photo on 29 July 1984 against the wall of the church. His daughter held the photo — hence her thumb at bottom left. Cheating seems to be excluded. We have not found an explanation for this photo; we simply submit it for further study, like the others. Inquiries are somewhat hampered by the fact that anyone in Yugoslavia who allows their name to be associated with Medjugorje is likely to attract unfavourable attention. R.L.

— Tobacco: 'You should not smoke more than five cigarettes a year' according to Professor Pujol, President of the Federation of Centres for the Campaign against Cancer.

— Alcohol is beneficial only if taken in moderation. For the adult a glass of wine 10-12 cm^3 during each meal, and for the child above the age of reason, a half finger of wine mixed with water ($\pm$ 5 cm^3), is what Professor Joyeux recommends. Keeping within this limit represents a healthy abstention without inconvenience.

Televison
The same principle applies to the artificial desires created by our civilisation: 'You should also abstain from television', the Virgin advised, according to Helena.

This abstention can only be beneficial. It would give an opportunity for silence and openness to God. Anyone who is in love will find the time for love. If we love God we will find the time for prayer. We have to borrow the time from elsewhere. Why not take the time that is uselessly spent in the mediocre activity of cultivating the television set, an activity that helps us avoid silence, and papers over the hidden sorrows and the anguish in our hearts. God is the remedy, the way to overcome it, the solution: not a stop-gap solution, for we who are made by God can find our fulfilment only in him. 'You have made us for yourself, Lord and our hearts will not find rest until they rest in you', says St. Augustine.

Meaning of fasting
Fasting is an irreplaceable means of meeting the challenge whereby, without denying our instincts, we assume them, discipline them, gain supremacy over them and go beyond them in placing our trust in God. That detachment which is acceptable in order to help us find God permits us to overcome the most basic egotistic and artificial attractions.

It leads us, through God himself, to the hundredfold promised by Christ in the Gospel. This hundredfold is given to the person who has overcome basic instinctive greed — well-ordered in the animal kingdom, and often out of control in humans — in order to find the very roots of that drive that leads to God. By overcoming egotism and the slavery of blind impulses we gain a better perspective of this world, inculcate a less possessive attitude towards the goods of this world and learn to use them more joyfully. It is the radiant attitude of joy shown in the life of Francis of Assisi. Whoever finds the world in God will find new and marvellous reasons for appreciating it as a gift of God: all things are beautiful. All are a gift from God.

This is equally true of food. Christ did not disapprove of festive meals. He began his ministry by changing water into wine at the marriage feast of Cana. He accepted the meals offered in his honour by converted publicans and sinners. He described heaven in terms of a festive banquet.

In the austere circumstance of the time, wedding feasts offered a rare period of free time, freedom, joy and a chance to meet others and share in the abundance. Jesus uses this very image to invite us to 'the table' of God himself (*Mt 8:11*). In fasting we discover the real value of the goods of this world. We really appreciate them when we are no longer their slaves. We are in a better position to accept God's gift if our lives are well-ordered and if we are capable of depriving ourselves in order to rediscover the essential. Dependence will then give way to freedom and openness to the essential.

A MEDICAL VIEW OF FASTING

A. What is natural or physiological fasting?

The period that follows the evening meal and precedes the first intake of food in the morning is the general point of reference in determining 'physiological fasting between meals', it could be stated that fasting ceases to be physiological, i.e. natural when the period since the last meal goes beyond sixteen hours. Strictly speaking it is during the second part of the night that physiological fasting takes place; during this period intake has been achieved, reserves are stored and the organism prepares to use its own reserves.

Nightly rest uses 500 calories
muscles: 200 calories, essentially lipoid in origin[5]
brain: 50 calories, essentially glucoside in origin
heart: 250 calories, essentially lipoid in character

B. What are the organism's natural reserves and its daily needs, apart from fasting?

1. Calories in reserve

Taking a man of 70kg as standard, we find 174,000 calories which can be broken down as follows.

Water + minerals	44.00 kg	=	0 cal
Glucosides	.50 kg	=	2000 cal
Proteins	11.50 kg	=	46000 cal
Lipoids	14.00 kg	=	126000 cal
	70.00 kg	=	174000 cal

2000 emergency calories are available immediately if there is no food intake. These calories are glucoside in origin and are stored in the liver. When these are used up the organism will call on its other reserves (protein

---

5. 1 gramme of lipoid = 9 calories; a gramme of glucoside = 4 calories.

and fat) which are found in the muscles and in the fat tissues beneath the skin.

We can thus say that a man needs, in proportion to his weight and height, from 50 to 100 calories per hour, or daily calorific need: 1200 — 2400 calories per 24 hours in proportion to weight and activity.

2. Daily calorific needs

The daily calorie intake should be broken down as follows:

15% protein or about 70 grammes

40% lipoids or about 100 grammes

45% glucosides or about 250 grammes

This calorie intake can be spread over the three meals as follows:

20-25% for breakfast

40% for lunch

30-35% for dinner

3. Liquid intake ought to balance water losses

1 to 1.5 litres in urine

0.1 litres in faecal matter

0.5 litres in evaporation

0.4 litres in perspiration and sweat (which can amount to several litres)

The daily water loss must be replaced.

C. What are the different forms of fasting from food?
1. Total fast for twenty-four hours

In this fast only water is taken. It is the primary phase of fasting which uses up the glucoside reserves in the liver; the reserves in the muscles begin to mobilise to take over from the depleted liver.

The brain needs 120-150 grammes of glucoside over twenty-four hours. This energy can only be supplied by the liver when the subject is on a total fast (water only). After twenty-four hours the immediately available reserves are depleted.

2. Reduced (half) fast

This was studied in the US in 1944 over a period of twenty-four weeks using thirty-two volunteers: the Minnesota Experiment. The experiment consisted of reducing the daily calorie intake to half while the water content remained the same (*Human Starvation*, Vols. 1 & 2, Minnesota Press 1950). In the follow-up the scientists studied the effects on the different reserves within the organism. This type of fasting is dangerous for the organism if undertaken for a long period.

3. Long-term total fasting (water only)

After the first twenty-four hours the secondary phase lasts from four to five days. When the sugar reserves of the liver are depleted, the body calls on other reserves (protein), in the first instance in organs such as the liver, spleen, intestine and then in the muscles. The tertiary phase begins at the start of the sixth or seventh day into the fast. This lasts for five or six weeks until protein reserves run out.

The terminal phase appears about the sixtieth day. It ends in death by malnutrition and respiratory failure following on atrophy and diminution of the muscles governing breathing. This is the outside limit of survival on such a fast.

D. What of a twenty-four fast on bread and water once a week?
1. Change in dietary habits
The consumption of bread and water only for twenty-four hours represents a definite change in our ordinary modern dietary habits. In fact it has been shown that the modern person's intake of calories, glucoside and lipoid, and of proteins (in meat in particular), is excessive.

— Individual intake of fats of animal origin is too high, representing as it does 40 per cent of consumption.

— The consumption of rapidly digestible glucose has increased: Sugar (cane or beet) consumption has risen from 20 kg per person per year in 1920 to 35 kg in 1975, the equivalent of 100 grammes per person per day. A balanced diet should not contain more than 50 grammes per day. Even if the quantity of raw sugar (lumps or granulated) has gone down, the amount of sugar contained in certain foods has increased: sweets, pastries, ice pops, ice cream, ready-made deserts.

— The consumption of syrup type drinks is too high, rising by 100 per cent in France from 1960 to 1980. They are an important source of rapidly assimilable glucose and therefore of calories.

— Consumption of bread has dropped by 50 per cent over the past forty years. It was 500 grammes per per person per day and it has now dropped to 150 grammes (1980). Contrary to popular opinion, bread is not fattening unless covered with butter or other fats.

2. Bread and water
Eating only bread and water for a period of twenty-four hours reduces the calorie intake to an average of 1000 calories: 50 grammes of bread = 25 grammes glucoside = 100 calories.
500 grammes of bread = 250 grammes of glucoside = 1000 calories.

Eating only bread provides very few proteins, lipoids (fats) and essential minerals (though there are more of the latter in wholemeal bread than in white bread).

Composition of the two most popular types of bread							
	Total Calories	Protein gr.	Glucosides gr.	Lipoids gr.	Calcium mg.	Sodium mg.	Magnesium mg.	Phosphorus mg.
White Bread	255	7	55	0.8	20	500	30	50
Whole-meal Bread	239	8	47.5	1.2	50	650	90	200

On reaching the stomach, bread remains there for two to three hours; water in general for less than one hour. On the day of fasting eating should be spread over the period; it is essential to spread the 1000 calories over the twenty-four hours.

Bread Consumption:
Five hundred grammes is a reasonable amount; a little more if required.

Water Consumption:
Normal intake should not be reduced; if anything it should be increased. We should be careful of this for there is often a tendency to reduce the water intake. In order to ensure proper dialysis and proper hydration it is necessary to drink a minimum of 1.5 litres of water. Again the intake should be spread over the day.

3. Effects of fasting on bread and water
If the fast is wisely undertaken — as indicated above, and apart from counter-indications — it will be well tolerated. The subject may feel hunger but will readily distinguish:

— hunger stimulated by the sight or smell of an appetising dish — we must just move away

— a real hunger which gives rise to weakness, pain in the back of the head and a heavy feeling in the head. This hunger can be satisfied with bread and water.

Sometimes fasting brings about hypoglycaemia — a lowering of the glucose level in the blood (below the normal level of 1 gram per litre).

The symptoms of hypoglycaemia are: headache, nervous tension, irritability, bad humour or painful sensations of hunger. More bread may remedy this. If the symptoms persist then fruit should be taken. Fruit provides simple sugars that are rapidly absorbed by the digestive tract and neutralise the hypoglycaemia.

Thirst indicates insufficient water intake. In winter it is advisable to drink hot water, particularly at breakfast. The amount should be increased in summer in order to compensate for the heat and more intense perspiration.

Fasting on bread and water may cause constipation if one does not drink enough water and even more so if the bread is wholemeal. The fibres facilitate intestinal transit provided there is sufficient water, but without the water they actually impede the process. For those who are subject to constipation fruit may help for two reasons — the water and the non-absorbed fibres which it contains. This periodic fast, during which the organism calls on its reserves, does not present any great difficulty but, on the contrary, stimulates a healthy elimination.

D. Counter-indications to fasting on bread and water
1. For the person in good health
One must rememebr that on the day chosen the calorie intake is reduced by half or even by two-thirds in the case of more active people.

— A climber would be strictly advised not to fast on the day of a long climb.

— A pregnant woman, or a nursing mother, should be strongly discouraged from fasting.

— A wood-cutter should not fast on a heavy work day.

— Technicians faced with delicate or dangerous tasks should not fast.

— The driver of a heavy goods vehicle with a twenty-four hour journey ahead should not fast.

2. The sick person
Fasting on bread and water should be forbidden in the case of the hospitalised or the convalescent. The chronically ill (apart from those suffering from over-nourishment), those suffering from cancer or from so-called systemic illnesses (illness of the collagen or the digestive tract) should not fast.

E. When a fast on bread and water can be undertaken
This fast is possible for people of all ages, male and female, after the age of puberty, although the elderly should consult a doctor.

Diabetics, those suffering from hypertension and obeseity, heart sufferers and those on special diets, may use this fast but only after prior medical consultation.

Extracts from a report on the measurement of spiritual energy associated with prayer

This report was completed at Medjugorje on 15-19 March by Mr Boguslav Lipinski, Boston.

The instrumentation
The instrument used for the recording of spiritual energy was originally designed for use in the field of nuclear energy: Electroscope, Model BT Biotech Canada. The unit measure is mR/Hr, milli rads per hour on a logarithmic scale that goes from 0-1,000,000. Normal background readings are from 0-15 mR/Hr.

Results and conclusion

Measurements were taken at Medjugorje over five hour periods, in different locations and at different times of the day. The highest intensity of spiritual energy was recorded on Friday 15 March; 100,000 mR/Hr. The most noticeable change in intensity was on Saturday 12 March during the apparition at the chapel at Gnobla.

1. The extremely high recordings during certain prayers (and their rapid disappearance) indicate a non-nuclear origin. For example the 100,000 mR/Hr recorded on 15 March would mean that people inside the church were being subjected to 100 rads per hour. The maximum permitted dose is 0.1 rads per day, in which case these people, who frequently attend Mass would be dead from post-radiation symptoms. But this is clearly not the case. We must therefore conclude that this energy has a spiritual origin.

2. This spiritual energy does not seem to bear any relationship to the numbers present but rather to the intensity and quality of their prayer.

3. There is no measurable change associated with the apparitions.

4. It is quite possible that the intensity of the spiritual energy is related to fasting. The highest reading was on a Friday.

5. The spiritual energy seems to cover a certain distance (1km) but it disappears rapidly: 5 to 30 minutes.

Questions requiring further study

1. Has this spiritual energy healing and protective properties? For example, there was no lightning in the Medjugorje area on 18 March while violent thunder storms raged in the surrounding mountains.

2. What is the physical nature of this spiritual energy?

3. Could the spiritual energy be detected by a different type of apparatus (Jaeger Miller)?

4. Is spiritual energy present in other locations during prayer, for example in the USA?

(There follows a table of 50 measurements taken at Medjugorje). In Buntic's house where he was lodging: 100-1000. In the parish church at 1.00 on 19 March there were only 20mR; there were 1000 on 18 March at 5.15; 10,000 at 6.00 p.m. and 20,000 at 7.00 p.m. and 100,000 during prayers in the chapel of the apparitions on Friday 15 March. As a point of comparison, in churches in the USA and at hockey matches the readings went from 20 to 70 mR.

Professor Lipinski, a specialist in bio-electrical phenomena, is researching cardio-vascular illness in Boston. He is studying radiation with reference to Einstein's theory on the unitary nature of energy: electro-magnetic, nuclear, gravitational. He is attempting to discover why the particular apparatus which records physical energy should react to spiritual phenomena associated with places of prayer and why, above all, he got unprecedented results in Medjugorje. He still has no answers to these questions.

3

Cures

It would be premature to present a balance-sheet of the cures at Medjugorje. We reported on them in *La Vierge apparait-elle a Medjugorje?* At that stage we presented a dossier of fifty-six cases prepared by Father Rupcic and Dr Mangiapan of the Medical Bureau at Lourdes. With his experience, Dr Mangiapan was able to make a quick categorisation, not between authentic and unauthentic cures — this would have been premature — but between those which had no chance of being confirmed according to established norms and those that would merit further attention: organic illnesses that could either be determined or had been diagnosed as such. We reported both sides of his conclusion.

— These claims of cures are of an indicative nature only, and do not allow any conclusion to be drawn.

— Many of them are of great interest and have a chance of being confirmed. Therefore, they invite further inquiry with a view to confirmation.

Dr Mangiapan developed both sides of his conclusion in April 1984 (Bulletin de L'AMIL — Association Medicale Internationale de Lourdes). He takes up the negative side in the first instance. The fifty-six cures listed in Fr Rupcic's dossier are 'described briefly, and are based uniquely on the evidence of those involved. They are never confirmed... by an objective medical examination (...) rarely is the duration of the cure mentioned... (nor) are the treatment, the diagnosis or the grounds for any prognosis indicated. In conclusion, if we are to follow the norms of the Bureau, this entire dossier is of no practical value and as such would not give grounds for an argument in favour of the apparition: In this 'non-official' indictment of the apparitions of Medjugorje, Monsignor Zanic quoted only this last sentence as the 'completely negative (verdict) of Dr Mangiapan on the cures of Medjugorje'. In this he was being true to his method: concentration on the negative aspects while ignoring the positive ones. With all due respect for Monsignor Zanic as a man and a bishop, truth obliges us to point out that Dr Mangiapan's negative statement was preceded by the following:

'The relatively high number of cures claimed should be paralleled with what Dr de Saint-Maclou, my predecessor, called, at the beginning of Lourdes, "the miracle of numbers". Nine cases would merit a more careful inquiry:

— the four cases of child illness (the speciality of Dr Mangiapan);
— the case of tumours (one in particular);
— finally, the case of kidney infection treated by dialysis; nine cases out of fifty-six are worthy of attention. "It is a good score", is what I wrote to the author (René Laurentin), "if this were to prove positive on the basis of a more objective analysis (April 1984, No. 205-206, p. 14-15)".'

We have already stated elsewhere the questions raised by Monsignor Zanic's polemic:

— Why does he continue to state that there are no dossiers on the cures when such dossiers, beginning with Dr Stopar's, have in fact been provided to him?

— Why have there been no inquiries on the part of the Episcopal Medical Commission into the many sick people cured, who give thanks for cures that are as amazing as they are unexpected?

— Why does the indictment speak only of those who came to pray at Medjugorje and subsequently died?

— Why does he not speak of those who were at death's door and who are perfectly well today?

The cures continue

Italian doctors from Milan University and some others are keeping a close eye on the situation. They have compiled a dossier comprising one hundred and thirty items on the cure of Diana Basile (about which more later), and they are in the process of compiling others.

I might add that I was lucky enough during my trips to have a chance meeting with other people who were cured after either a visit to Medjugorje or after prayers had been offered there on their behalf.

Beside the chapel of the apparitions I met Maria Brumec, who had suffered from a compression fracture of the eleventh vertebra for a long time and had been hospitalised in Maribor. She had worn a back brace since 1982. After palliative treatments which were of no benefit, she was cured instantly on 8 August 1983. The most recent X-rays of her vertebral column show no traces of lesions.

Cures and confirmation

It has in no way been established that all the 'alleged' cures, as they are now termed at Lourdes, are illusions, as the documents emanating from the See of Mostar would seem to presume. A number of people who have been cured continue to give thanks.

We do not presume to claim prematurely that these cures are proven or miraculous. It takes from six to thirteen years to reach a conclusion of this nature: this has been the time span involved in the recognition of miracles over the past twenty years at Lourdes. It is not to be excluded that the same number of cases might be recognised at Medjugorje during the fifteen years that separate us from the year 2000 when the apparitions at Medjugorje will almost have reached their twentieth anniversary (2001).

Debates of this nature, involving so many different viewpoints — the yogi and the commissioner, the mystic and the doctor, the believer and the judge — are often difficult within the Church. The critical preoccupations of the judge often tend to overlook the living realities of the people of God. In order to discern better the cures of Medjugorje it may be useful to recall the following: The process of the certification of cures, as established under Benedict XIV and further developed in this century, are noteworthy, from both the medical and theological viewpoints because:

— from the medical point of view they derive from the scientific period when a quasi-geometric proof of miracles was required. It used to be said: 'All it takes is the confirmation of one miracle and scientism is confounded'. However, we have now gone beyond those illusory pretensions. Nowadays science is much more modest. It argues within the limits of probability and is more acutely aware of the boundaries to its achievements and of the remaining ambiguities;

— theology is now much more aware of mystery and of the twilight zone in which we reach the transcendent in our lives: this includes miracles;

— miracles are not magic. Scientific study reaches its disconcerting limits with inevitable misunderstandings between the gropings of science, which are and should remain critical, and the thanksgiving of the cured person for whom all has been made simple in a body and soul made free.

The cure of Diana Basile

Since a cure is not merely a fact but an event in the lives of people, by way of example we will give a simple account of the cure of Signora Diana Basile which occured on 23 May 1984 at Medjugorje. This mother of three had been ill since 1972:

— blindness in her right eye (optic retrobulbar neuritis);

— impairment of the motor function rendering her upper and lower members impotent;

100

— total urinary incontinence which brought on perineal dermatitis.

The university hospital at Milan had diagnosed multiple sclerosis. The Bishop of course objects that the diagnosis of multiple sclerosis is never absolutely certain until an autopsy is carried out, *post mortem*.

However, Professor Thièbaut, who has spoken to me more than once about this difficulty, pointed to two cures of multiple sclerosis in Lourdes:

— Thea Angele (German) was cured on 20 May 1950, subsequently confirmed on 20 June 1961.

— Brother Leo Schwager (Swiss) cured on 30 April 1952, subsequently confirmed on 28 December 1960.

The history of the illness and the combined evidence of the tests convinced Thièbaut (a conviction which was shared by the international commission) that the diagnosis was confirmed. If nowadays we want to be more radical on the grounds that the diagnosis of multiple sclerosis is a 'challenge', then we would have to delete the two cures at Lourdes from the list of sixty-four that have been confirmed over the period of 127 years. However, no one see this as a possibility.

The diagnosis of Diana Basile was made unequivocally by Professor Spaziante, who is a non-believer. It was based on electromyographic tests (these measure reaction times through needles inserted in muscles) and on an analysis of her pathological state. We do not wish to anticipate judgement on this remarkable dossier which now has over 130 items (many more than the original dossier sent to Mostar). Clearly, the case cannot be thrown out *a priori* and, it is to be hoped that the episcopal commission, with the help of the leading people who treated the case and compiled the dossier, will carry out an objective examination.

What follows simply illustrates how the cures in Medjugorje gave rise to inevitable problems. We also wish to share the news which was good, indeed marvellous, for the woman who experienced it, and for her husband (who up to then was a non-believer) and children. Another family happy in giving thanks! The happiness of that mother whose illness had reduced her to tatters, could not leave us indifferent — no more so than can the cure of the man born blind. Should procedures or clerical mistrust impose on us the attitude of the doctors of the law with their morose acts of thanksgiving?

'Glory to God. We know that this man (cured by Jesus) is a sinner!'

'Glory to God. We know that the apparitions at Medjugorje are hallucinations!'

Confirmation of a cure requires a long time, perhaps 4-12 years, if one can establish a dossier. Silence is important until this final and improbable outcome.

Confirmation is like a tomb from which cures emerge mummified. As a Lourdes journalist put it — you only get the corpse of a miracle.

Modern medical doctors have shown a more welcoming attitude to the cure of Diana Basile than did the doctors of the law to the cure of the man born blind. Their very science provides a basis for their astonishment. Let us hope that the ecclesiastical authority will show the same openness which does not exclude, but rather implies a critical sense. May that authority accept in faith the event of grace, the contours of which are being sounded out by the medical profession.

Leaving aside for the moment the technical study which has just commenced and, without wishing to anticipate the judgement of the bishop of Mostar, we will give an outline of the case. It will of course be disputed but it deserves to be made known for it is well documented. Diana speaks like the man born blind in John 9:25 'I know only one thing, I was blind and now I see' — 'I was blind in one eye and invalided for twelve years', says Diana, 'and suddenly at Medjugorje I experienced an improvement in my health. I regained 10/10 vision in the eye that was blind and in the other eye, the good one up to now, I have 9/10 vision'.

Here, then, are some details of this cure which can be judged in conscience according to the medical dossier established in the university of Milan.

Synthetic account from the Specialist Clinical Institute of the University of Milan
Diana Basile, 43 years, was born in Platici (Cosenza) on 25 October 1940, Via Graziano Imperatore 41, Tel 02/6426813. Profession: secretary/administrator, employee of the Specialist Clinical Institute, Traumatology Centre, Via Bignani 1, Tel 026430141, ext 271. Married, mother of three children.

History of the illness
The first symptoms of the illness appeared in 1972: disgraphy of the right hand, shaking (making it impossible to write or to eat) and complete blindness of the right eye (optic retrobulbar neurosis). Multiple sclerosis was diagnosed in November 1972, by Professor Zazullo, director of the Centre for Multiple Sclerosis. Illness necessitated an eighteen-month break from work. After a joint examination by Dr Riva (neurologist) and Professor Rette (chief physiotherapist) suspension of all work for reasons of invalidity was recommended. However Signore Basile pleaded with them, 'Do not kill me', and she was allowed to undertake restricted duties. She was transferred from the department of radiology to another section where her tasks would be minimal. At this stage she could not bend one of her arms.

The patient has difficulty in walking — lack of synchronisation of the legs, rigidity of the right knee, and finds it hard to get to her place of work.

She has little or no use of the right arm except as a support and, probably for that reason, the hypertrophy of the muscles was never verified.[1]

The serious urinary incontinence which was present since 1972 now became total. This gave rise to perineal dermatitis. Up to 1976 the patient had been treated with a hormone, ACTH, which stimulated the secretion of the adrenal glands. After a visit to Lourdes in 1974, although the aneurosis of the right eye persisted, there was an improvement in her movements. This improvement allowed for the suspension of all therapy after August 1983.

After the summer of 1983 conditions again deteriorated rapidly (total urinary incontinence, loss of balance and of the motor function, trembling etc).

In January 1984 the psycho-physical condition of the patient deteriorated (she experienced a serious crisis of depression). Dr Caputo Gallarate visited her at home. He certified the deterioration and advised hyperbaric oxygen therapy, which was never completed.

A colleague from work (Natalino Borghi, a professional nurse at the same clinic) invited Signora Basile to join a pilgrimage to Medjugorje, organised by Dom Giulio Giacometti, of the parish of St Nazaro, Milan. The priest had warned that nobody should enter the sacristy of the chapel during the apparition.

Signora Basile's account

I was at the bottom of the steps near the altar of the Church at Medjugorje on 23 May 1984. Signora Novella of Bologna took my arm and helped me climb the steps. At that point I no longer wished to enter the sacristy. I remembered that a gentleman who spoke French had told me not to move from where I was. At that moment the door opened and I entered the sacristy. I knelt behind the door. When the young people knelt down together, as if moved by some force, I heard a loud noise, then I remember no more (neither prayer nor observation). I only remember great joy and I saw certain episodes in my life, which I had completely forgotten, pass before me as if in a film; for example I remembered being sponsor at the baptism of a child whose parents have now moved elsewhere and whom I had forgotten.

At the end of the apparition I followed the visionaries who went to the main altar of the church of Medjugorje. I walked straight like everyone else. I knelt down normally but was not aware of anything strange. Signora Novella of Bologna came to me crying. She said — 'Today I received a double grace. I accompanied you and I went to confession to Father Tomislav.'

1. In the final analysis, it was because the doctors gave into Diana's pressing requests to to back to work, that this deficiency was not followed up. This makes confirmation difficult.

The French gentleman, about thirty years of age (perhaps he was a priest as he wore a Roman collar) was moved and he too embraced me.

Signor Stefano Fumagalli, Consultant at the Tribunal of Milan (Via Zuretti 12) who travelled on the same bus came to me and said: 'You are no longer the same person. I wanted a sign, and it came from you. What a change!'

The other pilgrims on the same bus knew very quickly that something had happened. They embraced Signora Basile and they were visibly moved.

In the evening, on re-entering the hotel at Ljubuski, Signora Basile found that she was no longer incontinent and the perineal dermatitis had disappeared. The right eye, blind since 1972, had regained normal vision.

On the following day (24 May 1984) Signora Basile went on foot with the nurse Natalino from Ljubuski to Medjugorje (about 10 km). Though barefoot she had no signs of cuts or blisters. As a sign of thanksgiving, on the same day (Thursday), she climbed the hill of the three crosses (Crnica: place of the first apparition).

The physiotherapist, Signora Caia of the Maggiolina Centre, (Via Timavo, Milan) followed Signora Basile's case. On seeing her on her return from Yugoslavia, she wept with emotion.

Signora Basile said:

'All that has happened to me has caused a great spring of joy to well up within me. It is difficult to explain in words. I would have wept if I had seen someone with the same illness as myself, because it is difficult to communicate the necessity for inner truth. We are not only flesh and blood, we are of God, we belong to God. It is difficult to accept illness.

Multiple sclerosis struck me at the age of thirty, in the prime of life, with two children, I was empty. I would say to someone else with the same illness: Go to Medjugorje. I had no hope, but I said to myself: If God wants it thus, I will accept myself as I am. However, God must think of my children. Others ought to do what I should have done. I suffered.

At home everyone is happy, my children and also my husband who was practically an atheist. However, he said: 'we should return as a ''thanksgiving''.'

Today, 5 July 1985, Signora Basile was visited by the ophthalnologist from the specialist Clinical Institute of Milan and examination of her sight confirmed 10/10 vision in right eye which had previously been blind, although the left eye had only 9/10 vision.

This attestation was made in Milan on 5 July 1984 by the undersigned doctors:

L. Frigerio G. Pifarotti,
A. Maggioni D. Maggioni
Doctors at the Specialist Clinical Institute of Milan.

A study of the phenomena of lights

The phenomena of lights which have taken place at Medjugorje have influenced the rapid development of pilgrimages. Otherwise it is difficult to explain the thousands who have gathered since the third day, attracted by the unusual lights. Though it is difficult to admit, much less explain these phenomena, it is much more difficult to dismiss them. We have drawn up a preliminary inventory (updated in the December edition) with samples of evidence in *La Vierge Apparait-elle a Medjugorje?* (p. 165).

Reasons for scepticism
The phenomena of lights are disconcerting in their variety.

— Phenomena around the cross: a more or less distinct luminous column or silhouette of the Virgin which blots out the cross or, according to some witnesses, appears beside it. There is not necessarily a contradiction here as the phenomena were not reported on the same day. This is the most numerous category. (22 and 26 October, 19 December 1981, then 24 June (film by M. Desrippes) 16 and 17 August, 15 September — the most likely date for another film made by an Italian, which has been shown to the bishop but which, as yet, I have not seen).

— Analogous phenomena at Crnica (the hill of the apparitions), notably on 15 September 1981. (*La Vierge Apparait-elle a Medjugorje?*, p. 165).

— A similar phenomenon (rarer and less well-attested) in the area of the church (14 September 1983).

— Solar phenomena analogous to Fatima[1]: 2-3 August 1981 (Kraljevic p. 98) 16-19 August 1984 (evidence sent to me from Cologne by E. Wint), then notably on 25 November at 15.00 hours and 7 December,

---

1. 'The miracle of the Sun', a new manifestation at Fatima (13 October 1917), had a sequel at Tre Fontane (Salvatore Nofri *I segni nel sole. I prodigi del 12 Aprile 1980 e del 12 Aprile 1982 elle tre fontana, Rome*, Ed. Propaganda mariana (undated), *Signs in the Sun. The marvels of 12 April 1980 and 12 April 1982 at Tre Fontane, Rome*).

15.45, of which three photos have been published in *L'Informateur* (Montreal, 4 February 1985 p.17). Signora Tambascia filmed a solar phenomenon on 16 July 1984 and I am awaiting news of it.

— Finally, there was a fire without any sign of burning on the spot where the flames were seen, on 28 October 1981 and perhaps on two or three other occasions.

On all these matters there are only occasional pieces of evidence. Nobody gathered the evidence systematically or with any regularity. This lack of documentary precision will be a major obstacle to future study of these phenomena and it is to be regretted that the authorities did not appoint an archivist/documentator on the spot who would have made proper records. The difficulty is that the authorities are intent on stifling the facts and the local pastors have to meet the growing and almost impossible pastoral and spiritual needs.

In the parish bulletin for 19 December 1981 I noted the following:

> Over the past few days a white light was seen over Krizevac: a white figure beneath the cross; and after that the cross turned white. Today at 11.30 (a more distinct phenomenon) the cross was transformed into a thin white column, then it took on the form of a slim white figure of the Mother of God: like a silhouette, open arms that turned in different directions and in the end took the form of a T: a cross. Numerous witnesses in different places perceived this sign.

If the fervour with which certain pilgrims seek out these phenomena inclines us to scepticism, nevertheless we cannot disregard the evidence of precise and balanced people who have seen and recorded (photographed or filmed) negatives that raise questions and require an explanation.

Credulity in these matters is foolish. On the other hand the *a priori* dismissal of the events based on uncritical catch phrases — collective hallucination, auto-suggestion, thermionic or electrical phenomena etc. — has not helped to advance the cause beyond giving us new labels for ignorance! Here, as elsewhere, scientific study demands precise examination and certification of explanatory hypotheses, whether they be grounded in the natural or supernatural orders or simply on 'unknown causes' which, of course, is valid only for as long as the unknown remains unclarified. This presentation merely aims to provide certain significant facts which have come to our attention sporadically, in the hope that more qualified experts, in either psychology or cosmic phenomena of the lumuimous nature, would undertake to investigate the dossier.

Films shot live
Cameras have captured the most characteristic phenomenon: the one that took place around the Cross of Krizevac.

1. Nello and Angela Portorieri shot two very different sequences:

— the crowd in prayer, 25 June 1984, was struck by the appearance of a large star that appeared and disappeared above the hill of Krizevac. The film which was shot recalls the incident clearly for those who witnessed it. But it is not clear that this bright patch on the right background would prove anything to experts.

— 4 August 1984, from 7.30 to 8.00 a.m. they filmed the hill of Krizevac without the cross. The Bishop disagrees with the identity of the hill. We note the fact because it was observed by witnesses who did not film it on 25 June. We just note the dates in case the phenomena recur, thus affording an opportunity for filming under better conditions. Jean Louis Martin, an opponent who attributes no significance to these phenomena, has told me that he observed the momentary disappearance of the arms of the cross on six occasions.

2. Piero Sestini from Florence filmed an analogous phenomenon on 9 September during which the cross appeared and disappeared. Another item for the dossier, to be examined. Meanwhile, we reserve judgment.

3. Louis Desrippes from Bordeaux, who was outside the church at Medjugorje on 7 August at 6.00 a.m. was surprised by a luminous phenomenon on the hill at Krizevac. The cross disappeared progressively into the light. In place of the base of the cross a dull globe appeared and on this globe the silhouette of a very small (given the distance) and indistinct woman. He was able to discern an arm movement and, up to a point, a face. He went for his camera which he had left in the church and shot a two-minute sequence of the end of the phenomenon which had lasted for about half an hour altogether. He had to be sparing with his film as he was coming towards the end of the roll. On the other hand those who witnessed the phenomenon with him interfered somewhat by requesting a look through the telescopic lens of his camera. There were six people present. Five saw the phenomenon but apparently the sixth did not. Father Tomislav, who was passing by, stayed for a moment and observed the phenomenon with the group.

Louis Desrippes wondered if the film had actually captured this unreal phenomenon. It had. I, together with many others have seen the film with him. The film was shot through telescopic lens. Unfortunately, the beginning of the phenomenon is not recorded. But one can clearly see the dull globe with the little flashing silhouette on top of it. This flashing gave me the impression of rotation. M. Desrippes saw in this the arm movement, which he had seen while looking directly at the phenomenon. Finally, the globe disappeared while on each side of the luminous silhouette the arms of the cross appeared as the figure disappeared. The cross reappeared, clear and normal. It seems difficult to reject this phenomenon, taken unexpectedly and in good faith and fixed on the film. It would be interesting to have the view of expert meteorologists, to see whether or not they might be able to offer a natural explanation.

Some witnesses were struck by the similarity with the miraculous medal: luminous Virgin on an earthly globe. This classical image sums up well the message of Medjugorje: The Virgin of Light coming to the aid of a world in peril, instructing it to turn to prayer and conversion.

Photographs and various phenomena

In order to prepare the ground for experts who would be better equipped to judge these phenomena, I offer a few samples of photographs that have been given to me:

1. A first photo representing the white silhouette of the Virgin above the crowd in which (on the left as you look), the Virgin's hands and face, though not very distinct, are rosy brown in colour.

This is not a photo of the hill of Krizevac as was the film which we discussed above. The photographer wanted to take the crowd. The picture was given to me with the following note:

> The photos were taken on 14 September 1983 by a lady from Mostar. She was in the crowd, absorbed in prayer, on the left hand side of the church. It was only when the film was developed that she saw the Madonna and the cross dominating the world. Mr Renzo Rivoli, Via Archorola 137, 41100, Modena, reproduced the original which his daughter held against the wall of the church. Her fingers are visible at the bottom.

2. A second photo. Dr Zelijko (Ribavaran 55300 SL, Posesa, Yugoslavia) was near the church. From that point he was photographing the hill of the apparitions (Podbrdo and Crnica). On one of the photos he was surprised to find, not the countryside, but instead a vague profile which evokes the image of a lady with a veil. The original bistre print is most evocative. On the other hand an enlarged black and white print which Dr Zelijko sent me does not mean anything. The vague area becomes insignificant. The person who took the photo and his family saw in it a sign that has taken on a profound meaning in the evolution of their lives as Christians.

3. A surprising third photograph was taken by Louise de Wit-Demolder (Valleistraat 3010, Wilssele, Belgium) on 6 September at 18.00 hours. She was behind the visionaries and to their right. This is why the backs of the heads of Ivan and Marija and the lighted side face of Ivanka appear. In front of them is an intensely illuminated centrepoint. Though somewhat vague, the photo is rather nice.

The effect appears to be explained by a flash going off directly in front of Madame de Wit-Demolder at the exact moment when she was taking her photo. However, what is surprising is that in spite of the violent light of the opposing flash one can clearly discern the face and the aura of a lady in the same direction; one also sees the head and hands of another photographer as well asthe lens of his camera; behind them, again hanging on the wall, is the painting of Our Lady of Medjugorje. Normally, the violence of the flash should have eclipsed the outline of the objects nearby. A more competent examination might therefore be useful.

We would show much more reserve in respect of certain strangely eccentric photographs in which rays of light take the shape of a cross — sometimes rather pretty — which can be explained by the effect of direct light on the camera.

Towards a methodical study

In order to draw up parameters of research and to identify which specialists might best examine these documents one might look *a priori* for an explanation from three quarters:

— Psychological explanation based on subjectivity (excluded by photographs and films).

— Physical phenomena of a cosmic nature: Geomagnetic, thermionic, electro-frictional or tectonic. The sheer diversity and irregularity of these phenomena do not allow us to be more precise.

— Supernatural phenomena, whose natural foundations and meanings would have to be identified.

The good standing of luminous phenomena in the Bible invites us not to exclude the supernatural *a priori*. Indeed, the biblical examples are more varied and more disconcerting than the phenomena at Medjugorje: brands of fire that pass in the night among the sacrificial victims offered by Abraham, the burning bush, the many lights alluded to by the prophets, the Transfiguration... we conclude too readily that these phenomena are mere literary forms. In the same sense the signs in the heavens announced by Christ as heralding the end of time ...are we to exclude a realistic interpretation of these words?

The witnesses of the solar phenomena made a connection with Fatima where the miracle of the sun (13 October 1917) was observed by a crowd which included many non-believers.

Can God still speak to us today through light? An answer to this question would require a series of interdisciplinary analyses: a critique of the evidence, comparison of the events at Medjugorje with other known natural phenomena of light that have always attracted man's attention (rainbow, *aurore borealis*), and the luminous phenomena attested to in the history of the Church.

Let me repeat, we do not pretend to have provided a study. It would be desirable if we inspired a study, on the grounds that it is foolish to eliminate the phenomena on the basis of a catch-phrase: if such a study were to be undertaken it would have to be precise and far-reaching. Again, if such a study cannot be completed then at least it would be a good thing to set down the limits to any possible explanation just as we did in the case of the phenomenon of ecstasy, that is at one and the same time observable and baffling. The phenomenon is situated in a coherent physical reality but it refers to something else which somehow goes beyond our ordinary faculty of explanation.

Appendix I
Dr Stopar's inquiries

Dr Ludvik Stopar, psychiatrist and parapsychologist, is the first doctor to have carried out a methodical examination on the visionaries of Medjugorje during the ecstasy. He completed his general medical studies at Gratz, studied psychiatry and hypnotherapy at Berlin and parapsychology at Freiburg-in Br-ieisgau. He was director of the polyclinic of Maribor (Yugoslavia) for fifteen years.

A. Report addressed to the See of Mostar (December 1984)

1. Region, subject, aim

Region: 79456 Medjugorje, near Mostar.

Subject: The parapsychological events that have been taking place since 24/25 June 1981 when, for the first time, Mary appeared to six young visionaries: children between the ages of 11 and 18. Since then the visions have become daily occurrences. They take place at about 18.00 hours. The children see, converse with and listen to Mary who in turn gives them recommendations and advice and answers their questions. The duration of the visions is from 3-10 minutes.

Aim: Official statement of the facts and confirmation of the exceptional character of these phenomena, by the ecclesiastical commission of Mostar.

2. Explanation

What is parapsychology? It is a new science dealing with phenomena that go beyond the normal (manifestations) of the interior life. Paraphysics (metaphysics) is the science of abnormal phenomena in the material world (materialisations, levitations, psychokinesis...). The task of these disciplines is to examine such phenomena, to evaluate them, discover their causes and put them in specific categories — thus providing a deeper knowledge of these poorly understood phenomena of nature and of humanity. *Categorisation:* Animist phenomena (psychophysical) and transcendental phenomena (spiritualist), which are parapsychological or paraphysical, depend to a great extent (for their categorisation) on the psychologist's philosophical presuppositions. A materialist parapsychologist would deal with and categorise these phenomena in a different manner from an atheist parapsychologist. Similarly, a monist would deal with them in a monist fashion. I would class myself among the theist parapsychologists who recognise the transcendant.

It is the right and duty of parapsychology/paraphysics to examine these phenomena wherever they appear, including Christian mysticism, but in this case the evaluation belongs strictly to those charismatic mystics who have the gift of discernment.

112

The Psychosomatic Correlation

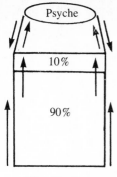

The Absolute

Source of
Good:
God

Source of
Evil:
Lucifer

In the psychosomatic correlation the psyche is influenced by God and by Lucifer. It has been established, through checking the bases and origins of such phenomena that: 10% begins in, or is influenced by the conscious level, and 90% begins in the deep subconscious level.

The 10% which is the conscious level has to do with reason, culture, intellect and environment, which are products of such factors as time, race, civilisation, religion, morals etc. The 90% subconscious includes intuition, inspiration, instinct, interior voices, animal life etc.

3. Application

The six visionaries of Medjugorje claim to see Mary objectively and corporeally in three dimensions: this is the kind of apparition where the visionary has the sensation of being in the presence of a living person. The sensations are objective and, as we said, they have been happening now for almost twenty months, every day at about 18.00 hours.

The psychosomatic state of the visionaries
Various tests — neuro-psychiatric, medico-psychologicaland somatological — have demonstrated that these children are normal. Given their age, their origins, their intelligence and their culture, their reactions are normal and offer no psycho-pathological indications.

4. Method

Objectivisation
The best method of detecting possible manipulation is medical hypnosis. By inducing trance, I separated the 10% conscious level. It was then the 90% subconscious which answered my questions. This level can only reproduce a real, lived experience, an experience gained through objective reactions which have been determined over twenty months and fixed in the layers of the brain.

Summary
It would be juridically unsound to reach an uninformed judgement based on indications that are fundamentally unproven, above all when dealing with parapsychological phenomena.

Conclusion

I request that an ecclesiastical commission be given a mandate by the authority of Mostar to open a canonical process which will examine objectively and establish rigorously that these parapsychological phenomena are theist and transcendent; that they are not the result of human manipulation.

Interview by René Laurentin with Ludvik Stopar (1982-1983)

RL — Why did you go to Medjugorje?

LS — Parapsychological phenomena are my line of work. I could not be uninterested in these events which have taken place in my own country.

RL — When did you go to Medjugorje?

LS — Four times: in May 1982, November 1982, June 1983 and November 1983. Each visit lasted from five to ten days.

RL — Your memorandum, written in German, was made known to me about a year ago. It was given to me under the seal of secrecy, but it is well known today and you yourself have published a summary of it in a Brazilian periodical. In this you claim to have separated the 90% subconscious from the 10% conscious level of the visionaries and in this way you have been able to establish their sincerity. What then was your method and on whom did you carry it out?

LS — Hypnosis, administered to Marija Pavlovic, who appeared to me to be the most intelligent and the most mature of the visionaries and who was therefore the most suitable for the test.

RL — Did you use touch, eye-contact?

LS — Neither. She closed her eyes. Once asleep, she breathes as if asleep. During the two previous days I had her give me her account of the visions without hypnosis. I asked her to repeat the account under hypnosis and she did this for one hour. While hypnotised only the subconsious level operated. The 10% conscious level was asleep. There was no difference between the two accounts; both were the same.

RL — You do not want to say that she gave exactly the same account, in exactly the same words?

LS — No, certainly not. She used different words but the meaning was the same.

RL — Were there other differences?

LS — In the early account, not under hypnosis, Marija kept the secrets confided to her by the apparition, very strictly. Under hypnosis she told them, to me.

RL — But surely, a violation of conscience! Now the secrets are no longer a secret?

LS — You can trust my professionalism. The secrets remain as secret for me as for Marija. I would not confide them, even to you. It is as serious as the seal of the confessional.

RL — When I questioned Marija about this hypnosis I was surprised that she does not seem to remember what she said to you.

LS — This is quite normal. Marija excused herself at the end of the hypnosis: 'Excuse me Doctor, I cannot understand what happened to me; I went to sleep while talking to you'.

RL — One thing did surprise me. When I asked, 'did the Doctor ask your permission?', she replied, 'No'.

LS — If I had asked I am sure she would have refused. In therapy one does not ask permission.

People do not realise the daily pressures that are put on the visionaries; they have become the centre of attraction at Medjugorje. It is a very dangerous situation. In order to cope they have to be extremely well-balanced psychologically (despite the sensitivity of some of them) and doubtless they must enjoy inner support. 'I met Dr Stopar in the sacristy, I thought he was a priest and for that reason I held a conversation with him', Marija told me.

There are risks involved with hypnosis. Dr Stopar took care to avoid them. Others may not.

The visionaries are subjected to surprises and even aggression more frequently than might appear, even at the level of the tests. We have already noted how Father Bulat prodded Vicka twice in the back with a large needle and caused a bloodstain that was visible through her clothing. He had not asked for permission; the memorandum of Father Rupcic recollects that sufficient precautions against infection were not taken. Perhaps he merely wanted to underline the fact that Father Bulat had the needle in his hand on entering the church and that he inserted it through the clothing? I do not know. But even if he were guilty of greater negligence who could have stopped him?

On 14 January 1985 the doctors from Montpellier had been requested to do an aggression test involving a knife. The person who had made the request appeared to attribute the refusal to cooperate with this incongruous test to a lack of objectivity. He did a similar test himself. He pushed two fingers violently towards Vicka's eyes while she was in ecstasy.

At the end of the ecstasy he said, in substance, to Father Slavko in the presence of a number of witnesses:

> 'You saw what I did, an experiment. It is very important. This contradicts all the medical tests that have been undertaken because the doctors who carried out the experiments believed the apparitions even before testing them. Vicka reacted. She reacts to external stimuli. She retains her instinct for self-preservation, contrary to what has been said.'

I was astonished at his reaction as reported to me, for it is clear that ecstasy does not cut one off totally from the exterior world; as we have seen, there are degrees of variations. For this very reason Dr Stopar is not keen on using the word *ecstasy*. We have said that ecstasy involves partial disconnection from the outside world which leaves the visionaries with useful reflexes in a manner that varies according to circumstances.

The finger test was recorded simultaneously on two video cameras, one on the right side of Vicka and the other face on. I looked at both of them at least ten times on an ordinary monitor. I saw no sign of a defensive reflex; no protest, no interruption of the regular movement of the lips during the conversation which Vicka was holding with the Virgin at that moment and no facial grimace. Was there a blinking of the eyes, as would be normal? It is probable, but in order to be sure a minute examination of the video on a larger screen would be necessary.

In an impromptu conversation with Slavko, the inquisitor argued from a precedent: 'A doctor from the episcopal Commission', he said, 'prodded Vicka and she reacted'.

We should correct this statement: it was a *priest* and not a *doctor* who did this test. He personally felt there was a reaction, based on the simple fact that when she was pushed Vicka returned to her normal position by a visible, functional movement as evidenced on the video-cassette. However, on examining this video taken from the front neither Professor Joyeux nor myself saw any facial alteration. Not one of Vicka's muscles moved. Nicholas Bulat admits that, placed as he was behind Vicka, he was unable to see her face (and he has not seen the video recording).

Perhaps the inquisitor projected onto Vicka that violence which he put in his own gesture. It would have been difficult to do what he did and at the same time remain an impartial observer. Somebody else should have been asked to carry out the test.

There is no point in further labouring this incident which was much spoken of at Medjugorje; it adds nothing to our dossier. We mention it here as an illustration of the aggression and the trials to which the visionaries are subjected. People should think of protecting them!

Let us return to the interview with Ludvik Stopar:

RL   —   **What are your observations and conclusions regarding the ecstasy?**

LS   —   **I would prefer not to speak of ecstasy because there is not total disconnection from the outside world; normal reactions continue.**

RL   —   **There is however some disconnection? The visionaries are, for example, insensitive to camera flashes?**

LS   —   **This is true. Once I stood between Marija and the apparition. She did not appear to be disturbed. She did not attempt to push me out of the way. At the end of the apparition I said to her: 'You did not see her, I was between you and her'. She replied: 'That is the reason why I saw her in a light haze'. (The corpulent doctor had been reduced to the state of a cloud!).**

RL   —   **I would call it ecstasy because normal perceptions cease in favour of perceptions that are foreign to our world, because we do not see what they see. Do you have a name for that state?**

LS   —   **Yes. The perception of the outside world is diminished. Equally their sensitivity. But I know of no technical term to cover that particular state.**

RL   —   **It seems to me that there can be no image of the Virgin on the retina of their eyes, since the others present see nothing.**

LS   —   **I have not verified this fact, but it does seem evident to me as well. I can only tell you that the pupil is dilated. On the other hand, the visionaries insist on the reality of the vision. They see it in three dimensions. They can touch it. During the ecstasy a doctor asked Vicka to outline the Virgin. She took his hand and guided it around and then behind, thus indicating a third dimension.**

RL   —   **This does not get over the simplistic dilemma: subjective or objective? In my book I attempt to show how a being that does not belong to our cosmos could show itself objectively in a different fashion. Have you made other observations?**

LS   —   **I observed the lip movements of the visionaries during the ecstasy. They spoke coherently. But you could hear nothing. I said to them: 'How do you "extinguish" your voice?' They were astonished and replied: 'We speak normally.'**

The doctor seemed to think that there was only one conversation. I am now certain that during certain periods of the apparition a number of visionaries speak together and hold different conversations simultaneously. I showed him a number of photos that establish this fact.

RL   —   **An examination of the dated photos gave me the feeling that the visionaries became more and more relaxed, natural and transparent in the ecstasy. They were more deeply moved and more tense in the earlier periods.**

LS   —   **Yes, at the beginning they were endeavouring to adapt. Now they are more at ease, more at home in the state of ecstasy. You have no doubt observed as I have that the Virgin prays with them. She says the Our Father, never the Hail Mary. One is surprised when the voices return at hearing the six begin with perfect**

116

synchronisation, 'who art in heaven.' It is the Virgin who intones the first words, 'Our Father', they explain after the ecstasy.

RL   —   Have you had any difficulty with the police during your examinations?

LS   —   No, my freedom to undertake scientific research was respected. Perhaps they thought I would discover a fault. I was questioned only at the hotel: 'Where are you going, what are you doing...'?

RL   —   Do parapsychologists react differently to these phenomena in the spiritual world?

LS   —   There are three different approaches: the first, atheist; the second, Christian; the third based on the hypothesis of unknown forces. I am also interested in unknown forces but my approach is theological and I had the impression of coming into contact with a supernatural reality at Medjugorje.

Appendix II
Diabolical and other explanations

What if it was the devil?
This hypothesis has been put forward by three priests, one of whom has published his views, while the other two, more prudently, have kept their views private. However they were good enough to let me and other authorities have these views.

Satan disguised as an angel of light
We might well ask, 'Should this be a cause of scandal?' No, because Satan can, according to St Paul, disguise himself as an angel of light (*2 Co 11:14*) and two thousand years of Christian history bear witness to this. Bernadette considered this hypothesis, probably suggested in the family circle, after the first apparition. For this reason she brought a bottle of holy water to the second apparition and sprinkled Our Lady with it. The visionaries at Medjugorje did the same thing and were reassured by the same smile.

Saints who have been favoured with particular tangible graces, together with their spiritual directors, have retain a certain scepticism with regard to exceptional phenomena, situated as they are on that ambivalent frontier which is subject to illusion and temptation. It was proper that the hypothesis should be considered.

We do not wish to enter into a polemic with the protagonists of the hyptheis. It would merely serve to exacerbate the situation and increase the unhealthy preoccupation with the spirit of darkness. It is better to adopt the humorous attitude of St Thérèse of Lisieux who pictured herself chasing the devil in the family cellar where he hid himself behind the barrels. I will respect the anonymity of the three protagonists (all independent) knowing that a polemic can wound the adversary and stifle debate. I respect the intelligence and even the integrity of those who have developed this thesis; at times I have to admire the dexterity with which they can highlight even the smallest detail.

What is lacking is first-hand knowledge of the facts: the visionaries, the ecstasy, parish life, the admirable movement towards conversion, the innumerable attestations (oral and written) of these conversions, which are the principal elements in this debate according to the Gospel saying, 'a tree is judged by its fruit'. It is illusory to attempt a second-hand examination of Medjugorje, purely at the level of dialectical argument and without any critical examination of the sources.

Another weakness in these intelligent studies is their systematic and polemic nature. This leads them to discover in the slightest detail, in the smallest complaint, dark and infernal indications that do not make sense in the light of the facts. I do not claim that there have not been mistakes and weaknesses at Medjugorje; I fear in fact that these weaknesses may be aggravated in the tense situation of a parish that is not only not helped by episcopal authority but is constantly placed in impossible situations that multiply the risks of error and deviation. In such conditions I have great admiration that up to now such good sense has prevailed or, at least, that mistakes have been rectified.

Finally, the dialectical method used to discover the Devil at Medjugorje consists of stringing together a number of most unusual studies, all guided by the initial hypothesis, thus tying in minute details to suit the pre-established position. The method is attractive, but artificial.

Where it is said that Fr Laurentin does not quote such and such a statement, recall such and such a fact, why does he hide them? (for what subterfuge, what dishonest motives? etc.) — usually it is because I had no definite proof or, indeed, because the fact or statement was of a secondary nature; I retained only the essential in a book of 198 pages. It was not a book of 1000 or 2000 pages and yet it dealt with over 1000 apparitions. Discernment comes through contact with people and the places that is why I returned so often to Medjugorje.

The objectives
To go beyond the realm of the abstract let us examine the objectives:

1. One of the protagonists who was somewhat embarrassed by the use of holy water, which, because of the precedent at Lourdes, has a certain positive value, asked the question: 'But where did this holy water come from; was it properly blessed according to the rites of the Church etc?' He honestly admits that he has no answer to this question. Not wanting to enter into the system and without wishing to prove anything, unlike the intrepid protagonists of diabolical intervention, I am in a position to offer him details which he can use in his own favour. The holy water which was brought by Marinko (protector of the visionaries, father of an admirable family and an excellent technician) was not taken from the holy water font but from a neighbour's (Vicka's) house.

> 'At home,' Vicka says, 'we still sprinkle holy water both inside and outside the house as we have done since my childhood according to tradition; this water was made (according to an ancient tradition dating back to the Muslim persecutions) by putting blessed salt in the water and reciting the Credo.' (Bubalo, p. 27 and personal inquiry)

One might ask if such water had the power to chase away the devil. Is it not, as it were, counterfeit holy water? No. It is simply a local tradition accepted and maintained by the priests (a tradition that is falling into disuse). Parishioners do not get their holy water from the font but they do require salt that has been blessed by the priests. It is not therefore simply a lay blessing. It is holy water blessed according to a tradition of the local church, requiring the prayerful participation of the laity (in the recital of the Credo) all of which is to the credit of this popular rite of Hercegovina. There is absolutely no basis for calling this practice into question.

2. A weightier argument: the Virgin recites the Our Father and the Gloria with the children every day, as we have seen. The fact that she does not recite the Hail Mary, just as she did not at Lourdes, is a positive indication of authenticity. But the diabolists object: 'If the Virgin says "forgive us our trespasses... lead us not into temptation, but deliver us from evil", then she is praying as if she were a sinner. These apparitions stain the stainless one, the Immaculate. Diabolical influences are thus evident.'

In the first instance we should note that Christ himself pronounced the Our Father in teaching his disciples. It cannot be precluded that he repeated it with them, for them, in their name.

On the other hand, one cannot say that the Virgin did not recite the Our Father at Lourdes. Early evidence is very strong on the fact that her lips did not move while reciting the rosary. Estrade (alone) said much later on (1878) that she did recite the Gloria, but provided no information about the Our Father, positive or negative.

At Medjugorje Mary recites the Our Father with the visionaries in order to teach them to pray this prayer. If she recites the first part in her own name and in the name of the whole Church, without distinction, she recites the second part in the name of all those still in the earthly condition. It is for us, for the entire Church of which she is the prototype and the first member, that she asks what she herself no longer needs 'lead us not into temptation, but deliver us from evil' and, what for her never had an object, 'Forgive us our trespasses'. There is no reason to believe that Mary remained silent in the primitive Church when the Our Father, taught by Jesus, was being recited. No doubt she said it in its entirety with, and in, the community, implying the word 'us' the holy Church which is made up of sinful members; this made sense before God and for her, according to a truth which she did not analyse. It would be foolish to speculate on the meaning she gave (intuitive rather than reflective) to the words of that prayer. This type of objection was made use of by the scribes who tried to trap Jesus in his speech.

The visionaries whom I questioned at Medjugorje see no problem in this. 'Our Lady says "us" for all', says Jakov. In other words, in our name.

Christ himself, 'whom God made into sin' (*2 Co 5:21*), prays for the Holy Church, made up of sinners, in the name of sinners for whom he died and who are, moreover, his body, identified with him as his mystical body. We should not minimise Christ's and the saints' solidarity with sinners, in view of their conversion.

3. They believed that there was a 'pernicious error' in Vicka's reply to this question from Father Tomislav: 'Do you experience the Virgin as she who dispenses graces or as the one who prays to God?' — 'As the one who prays to God,' Vicka answers.

'To reduce our Lady Immaculate, Mother of God, our mother, mediatrix of all graces and coredemptrix to the exclusive role of one who prays, on the same footing as the faithful, is this not a scandalous and diabolical amputation?' — they ask.

No, I am rather more astonished by the question — reminiscent of the question which was sometimes put to children: whom do you love the more, your mother or your father? Clever children were able to avoid the question. But Tomislav Vlasic's question was not intended to exclude anything. It merely sought the weight given to an aspect. Now, that adoration, total deference to God, should be the dominant feature of the Virgin is self-evident and this is recognised in Vicka's response. This does not exclude the fact that with God and in God she comes to our aid. In fact this becomes all the more clear by putting the fundamental and heaviest emphasis on her total deference to God.

Medjurogje was suspect for another reason: mariolatry, notably in connection with the prayer of consecration to Mary inspired by Helena, 19 April 1983: 'Out of your love and your grace, save me; I desire to be yours and love you infinitely'. It is objected that only to Christ can one say 'your grace'. This complaint is the exact opposite of the previous one: the place of Mary both as creature and adorer seems to be forgotten. She is transformed into a goddess. The devil is again present, this time because of the presence of an error that is diametrically opposed to the previous one.

I do not believe that Helena's formula is the best in the world. I would have preferred if these formulas had greater sharpness and clarity and made more explicit reference to Christ. But this reference to Christ is not really forgotten. With Helena it is often very explicit.

In the same prayer she says to Mary: 'I beg you to give me the grace to be merciful towards you'. More than one theologian has raised an eyebrow at this rather strange expression. How would a child have to be merciful towards the Virgin? Helena's words should be understood in the context of her intimate dialogue with Our Lady. Her spiritual ambition sometimes led her to make indiscreet demands: for example she wanted to share the secrets revealed to the visionaries. The Virgin answered: 'Excuse me, but that I cannot give for it is not the will of God'. The absolute primacy of God appears in the most explicit way possible at the end of this response. And the first words, 'excuse me', words of exquisite courtesy, warn Helena against that sulkiness into which some Christians lapse if God does not instantly grant them some grace which they ask.

5. A short saying from our Lady on ecumenism likewise caused some to crib, those who complain about the ecumenism of Vatican II and who blame Medjugorje for being in line with the Council.

> 'In God there is neither division or religion. It is you in the world who have created these divisions. The only mediator is Jesus Christ. There are divisions because believers have become separated one from the other. Do not make distinctions between people'.

Some saw indifference here, arguing also from another saying which I do not believe to be well established: 'God directs all confessions as a king his subjects, by his ministers'. (According to the context, which is not clear, 'ministers' could be angels rather than the ministers of the various religions.) The argument runs that in this case all religions would be equal, of equal value. In fact the same message says exactly the opposite: 'The fact that you belong to one religion or another is not without importance. The Spirit is not equally present in each Church'. On the same day one of the visionaries heard the following declaration which leans in a Catholic and apologetic direction: 'You see that all apparitions take place in the Catholic Church; they ought to say a lot to you'.

The difficulties here are created by removing the message from its context. The vital context, of central importance, is the message of reconciliation. The Balkans, a country of many divisions, is experiencing impossible tensions. For the Christians themselves (marked by centuries of persecution and hemmed in by an atheistic regime) the invitation 'to love your enemies', as the Gospel says, i.e. those towards whom (by custom or spontaneously) they harboured enmity and acrimony, is new and full of meaning. In Bosnia-Hercegovina the Muslims converted many to Islam. Hostility reigns and both groups despise each other. There is similar hostility between the Catholic Croatians and the Serb Orthodox. The invitation of Our Lady is to unbounded love which will reach beyond all the antipathy ingrained in their customs. 'Love your Croatian brothers who are Muslims, the Orthodox Serbs and the communists who persecute you. Respect all persons'.

I see nothing dialobical in any of this; it is a faithful echo of the Gospel. Let us not imitate the erudite and brilliant intelligence of the Scribes who attacked Christ's proposals with unparalleled zeal; the defects of this group were surmounted by Nicodemus and Joseph of Arimathea.

If the Muslims and Orthodox come to Medjugorje they should be made welcome; this marks progress towards the reconciliation which the message aims to promote. This seems suspect only to those who wish for a Christian triumph through religious or political war and not through God or through charity, in accordance with what is written in the Gospel.

It is in this context that we ought to situate other statements which have been incriminated:

— Respect the Muslims and the Orthodox Serbs. You are not Christian unless you respect them.

— Respect each person's religion and preserve your own intact for yourselves and for your children.

Mirjana insists that what the Virgin says is that we are all equal before God. 'She said that all persons are equal before God and not that all religions are equal'. We are equal as people.

Thus, it is clear that objections (and others which are more subtle) are based on estimations of the formula, rarely liberal, in which the visionaries give the words of Our Lady, and on biased and malevolant interpretations. The Christian rule in such cases is to understand each proposal within the overall context and to explain any difference in language in terms of the general context. The doctrinal context of Medjugorje is beyond reproach, according to a declaration by Mgr Franic, president of the Yugoslav Episcopal Commission on Doctrine, a man reputed to have belonged to the conservative minority group in the Council and a close friend of Cardinal Ottaviani. Helena's tender love for the Virgin could sometimes give the impression of mariocentricity which, however, is not suspect when one notes her essential and fundamental reference to Christ.

A trap avoided through lucidity
We must go further. According to tradition and the experience of Christian mystics, the visionaries recognised and overcame the pitfalls of pride and the devil.

One day, at the time of the apparition, Mirjana saw the light that precedes the apparition but in the light, under Mary's garment's, the Tempter appeared, offering her flattering promises of happiness in this world if she listened to him. She did not allow herself to be taken in.

To see in this temptation uncovered and overcome a sign that all the apparitions were of the same nature would be to ignore the traps which the great mystics recognised and overcame.

The diabolical at Lourdes?
The diabolic hypothesis, brilliantly developed by an ingenious collage of unchecked texts, is part of the system. It emerges inevitably in these cases.

At Lourdes several priests subscribed to this theory. Father Nègre, an erudite Jesuit, revered for his piety, admonished Bernadette at length on the point:

> 'My poor child, you have seen a lady? You have seen the devil! 'Bernadette turned towards me,' the witness Antoinette Tardhivail recounted, 'and she said to me':
>
>> "the devil is not as beautiful as that."
>> "Tell me little one, you have not seen his feet? One does not see the feet of the devil."
>> "Oh yes, she was barefoot, very pretty."
>
> He maintained that this was false; she remained peaceful and calm.
>
>> "But you did not see the hands. They are hidden by a shodow!"
>> "No, I saw them and they were very pretty."

The tone of voice of the priest indicated that the vision was false. He gave a long dissertation on the deformities of the devil. He refused to believe that Bernadette had seen the hands and the feet (Evidence of Antoinette Tardhivail in René Laurentin, *Bernadette vous parle*, Paris, 1972, vol. 1, p. 179).

He admitted later on that he had had this conversation with Bernadette in Madame Pailhasson's home between 20 July and 20 August 1858. His conviction was based on this principle: God does not allow the devil to take on the complete human form. The devil always hides the hands and the feet (reputed to be cloven and those of a beast). Thus he was forever looking for a new zone of shadow into which he could slot the devil whom he had brought along as part of his baggage. One always finds a shadowy zone into which the devil can be slotted.

It is all the more easy given the fact that apparitions and charisms, tangible manifestations of God in concrete human life, are not always unambivalent. These tangible graces awaken and release human and imaginative forces. The visionary may well be able to call on energies hitherto unknown and to use these energies for the wrong purposes. The Tempter is quite capable of stimulating deviant actions in this area. For this reason visionaries and mystics have always needed humility and have relied on spiritual directors. It is therefore regrettable that the authorities should put difficulties in the way in the case of the parish at Medjugorje which neither facilitate a balanced approach nor promote in-depth growth. In these conditions a permanent miracle is required if certain deviations are to be avoided.

In order to take a more accurate measure of the diabolical interpretations of Medjugorje I have endeavoured to develop a counter-position. Were we to apply the same method to Lourdes, La Salette, Fatima: seek out the worst, exploit every ambiguity or implication, Lourdes would have been much more vulnerable than Medjugorje. Bernadette's penitential gestures: kissing the ground, eating grass, would certainly have scandalised the devotees of the apparitions and embarrased the commission. 'You have eaten grass like the animals', they said to Bernadette. 'This sordid gesture is not worthy of the Mother of God and (not in keeping with) human dignity.' 'But we eat salad', she answered ingenuously.

The most serious problem at Lourdes was the epidemic of false visionaries who invaded the Grotto of Lourdes from 11 April to 11 July, 1868. Bernadette was forgotten. Estrade himself, who had become infatuated with Josephine Albario, proclaimed during one of her pseudo-ecstasies: 'those who will not believe are rabble!' (as was noted by a member of the commission on the same day).

The first of the false visionaries, unlike Bernadette, who never went to catechism classes until she was fourteen, enjoyed the reputation of being pious young ladies, beyond reproach, children of Mary. They were welcomed by Fr Peyramale far more than Bernadette. Mayor Lacade's maid, Marie Courrech, held the attention of the commission briefly. Mgr Laurence, with the help of a remarkable commission, had the good sense to burst that particular bubble: they rediscovered the forgotten Bernadette and consigned to oblivion even the best-known of the visionaries who had followed her from April to July.

If there had been more than fifty visionaries at Medjugorje as there were at Lourdes, what a triumph it would be for the protagonists of the theory of the intervention of the devil!

It is true that the Bishop of Mostar claims to have forty-seven visionaries in his diocese. To my knowledge, none of them operates in public. Priests have had to dispel one or other illusion either in the confessional or through spiritual direction. There are no others in the chapel of the apparitions or with the visionaries, as there were in the grotto at Lourdes. I have established the list of the forty-eight who are known by name (*Lourdes, Documents authentiques*, vol. 2, pp. 58-78) to which should be added the groups of anonymous 'visionaries' (listed ibid., pp. 78-96).

Conclusions

What emerges from these dark and gloomy interpretations of Medjugorje is the fact that the best apparitions are never presented as absolute evidence. The Church itself, which teaches the faith and pronounces with the absolute authority of God, does not claim the same assurance when she exercises discernment or judgement in respect of apparitions.

The reason for this is that this tangible incursion of the supernatural, which arises as a special grace, a support or stimulus for faith, is always given in a certain twilight zone. Private revelations are never super-revelations but rather a modest reminder of the one and only revelation. This stimulus strikes the sense faculties of the beneficiaries, according to the circumstances of place and of time, as well as those of the visionaries themselves — according to the visionaries' measure, *ad modum recipientis*, as the thomistic phrase puts it. Apparitions of Christ or of the Virgin are not the beatific vision; the absolute intuition of God. It is a modest communication, through signs that are adapted to the limits and capacities of the receivers. Let me repeat, when we speak of signs it is not to suggest that the apparitions are artificial images. We simply take into account the fact that all our knowledge on this earth is achieved through signs, with all the relativity of all the signs involved in human knowledge: colour or sound, transmitted by vibrations of certain wavelengths, and the concepts which the mind develops from these data. This is the humble status of all human knowledge, forever complex and relative. Apparitions are bound up in this complexity. The garments of the Virgin (which vary from Lourdes, Fatima and Medjugorje) are relative, as are her height and her age. These are not important: a glorified body transcends the succession of ages. The signs involved in the apparition do not hide it; they manifest it. They do not come between us and the vision, they transmit it. They are not an illusory veil, they are transparency. Their only function is to make known what (whom) it is that appears, as in the case of every other sign, though these belong to a different order (or existence).

From this sombre dossier, with its proneness to extrapolate and over-distil the smallest of details, what does remain constant is the humility of this means of communication. The visionaries, with all their strengths and admirable naiveté (naiveté is a quality, sometimes akin to genius, in a visionary as in an artist), do not behave as magicians or fortune tellers or guadians of the absolute, but rather as beneficiaries of a unique encounter which transcends them and is responsible for the light and benefits that accrue to them and others.

They are absolutely convinced of what they saw and would lay down their lives rather than deny it. But they know their own limits. When Father Tomislav asked Mirjana: 'You said that these apparitions would be the last on this earth, what did you really mean? Are they the last for this period of the Church or the last for ever on this earth?' Mirjana did not pretend to be qualified to interpret this. She answered: 'I do not know, she said it was the last apparition on this earth. I do not understand beyond that'. On a further question by Father Tomislav: 'Other visionaries have told me: the last apparitions for this period of the Church' (and not until the end of time). Mirjana held firm: 'I do not know. She said she would not appear again on earth. 'I do not know if this means in this era. I did not think that I should have questioned her on that subject.'

These messages call for interpretation, a hermeneutic, an exegesis, as it is called. If Scripture needs interpretation (as does any human language or message) all the more so do these messages handed on candidly and without sophistication by young people who repeat as well as they can what they have understood. Their preoccupation is to pass it on and to live it, not to speculate on words. They understand what they receive in the very act of living out their lives in dedication to God. They do not attend to literal precision and they usually recount the sayings in indirect style and in their adolescent language, without affectation. We should avoid hardening or making absolute their proposals, above all where they deal with controversies. This happened where the questions dealing with the two Franciscans who were experiencing difficulties with the bishop of Mostar were repeated over and over again (thirteen times).

On the other hand the encounter is largely a contact between these adolescents and their mother; doubly a mother in the case of two of them who are orphans. Contact between a mother and child has nothing to do with literature. It is on a different level. At the human level the baby talk between mother and infant, before the child can talk, is what is most fundamental in our initial formation. But no one would ever think of editing it, not even in those families where archives are kept. Tens of thousands of pages would be filled with the 'conversations', liberally sprinkled with onomatopoeia, from the first one or two years. The result would be insipid and weak, without the smiles, the mimes, the human warmth. It is not always thus with the language of love! And this communication is so true, so formative and so edifying!

How these young people are growing in health and holiness! It is pointless to record their daily conversations for they simply repeat a message of prayer, conversion and charity. One could criticise the monotony of all mothers' conversations with their children if we merely spectate from the outside.

'If I saw this lady every day for two years I would be bored by now', a theologian from Zagreb said. 'So would I', answered one of the visionaries, 'if it were not for love'. I never cease to admire the fruits of this loving exchange every time I see the visionaries coping so well with the entanglements of impossible situations, politely, with good humour, great tact and constant charity. Compared to them I feel very small in the eyes of God. Their health and holiness show the marks of the humility incubated by Our Lady and this is not the least of the signs of authenticity. May we know how to recognise the gift of God without excessive proof.

A bishop informed me that certain members of the Commission, those most able at compiling objections, at one time put forward the hypothesis that the apparitions were a plot by the marxist government aimed at discrediting the Church. I will not give any names. However, such a hypothesis shows the absurd ends to which critics will go when, instead of ascertaining they suppose, instead of evaluating they deprecate, and, instead of discerning they systematise. If Marxism could play so well at being Christian it would be converted, as was Constantine of old. If the devil could lead so many people to faith, to prayer, to conversion, to the confessional, to fasting, to pardon and to reconciliation, then the devil would be converted.

Let us respect the serious intent of the adversary, whether we are dealing with atheists or with Satan.

> It is only by Be-el'zebub, the prince of demons that this man casts out demons. (*Mt 12:24; Mk 3:22; Lk 11:25*)

> Are we not right in saying that you are a samaritan and have a demon? (*Jn 8:48*)

Conclusions

The scientific studies and approach of this volume indicate, within their limits — and each one according to the stage at which it is — the interest in and the serious import of the *fact* of Medjugorje. Its serious Christian and spiritual import rests on clear bases which the studies have either helped to highlight or on which they have invited further scrutiny. Science is research. It does not comment; it opens files which we should not close too hastily. Nevertheless we offer a first summary judgment of this study — still ongoing — of the facts of Medjugorje.

1. The visionaries are psychologically healthy, without neurosis, or hysteria. Their ecstasies are not a pathological phenomenon. We are not dealing with hallucination or a morbid accident. It is a functional phenomenon[1] which conditions a valuable experience: one which is coherent, healthy, enlivening and, for the visionaries, both human and spiritual. The scientific tests do not explain this experience. They discoverthe paradox of an objective communication independent of the ordinary sensory pathways. This statement does not give the lie to the evidence of the visionaries, rather it sets it within a positive framework. These young people live out an encounter which is in itself, in many respects, the most obvious explanation of the phenomenon, at a level which is evidently beyond science. The medical study neither proves nor contradicts their evidence. It verifies the contours. Above and beyond the tests, Christian spiritual criteria (stability, prayer, charity, holiness, the progress of these young people and the abundance of spiritual fruits) indicate an authentic encounter.

2. The fast on bread and water which hundreds of thousands of Christians have undertaken once or twice a week, according to the message of Medjugorje, is a fruitful experience.

Medically it is healthy and reasonable. The reduction in intake helps to counteract our excesses without any risk of starvation. A vegetarian diet corrects a diet of meat and of animal fats which multiplies cancers, as the recent studies of Henri Joyeux have shown. A reduction in those excesses, which it would take decades to bring about, would reduce by

---

1. Quite recently we examined M. Englebert's video, frame by frame, to check the simultaneities. On the evidence of a number of ecstasies (27, 28 December and 20 March), the first movement of the lips is simultaneous, though Jakov's voice, apparently at full volume, is the first to be audible, while Marija's returns progressively. Where they kneel down, simultaneity is less clear; Jakov's reaction time is quicker and Marija's slower. A quantified study ought to be undertaken.

half the number of cancers of the digestive system. Fasting is a step in the right direction in this sense.

From the Christian and spiritual point of view, fasting is above all the sign, the means and the vindication of a return to God. It facilitates openness to the essential, to prayer and hunger and thirst for God and for justice. From this point of view it could be a means of reconciliation between humanity and God and between each individual with others. This fruitful experience is a positive outcome of Medjugorje. This book hopes to help the process by indicating certain counter-indications and by pointing out the best way to fast.

3. The cures of Medjugorje are also a fact if we compare them to the cures at the outset of Lourdes or Fatima. The proportion, both in quality and quantity, is not smaller. These cures continue as we have shown. In briefly recalling the facts that have been hidden under a bushel we wish to provoke a study that would be worthy of the name. As yet, it has not been undertaken by the Episcopal Commission of Mostar. The doctors from the University of Milan have made a remarkable beginning. The friction between their scientific approach and the systematically suspicious critique which attempts to refute these cures without examination is an invitation to further elucidation of the underlying problem, thus establishing the question on a sounder basis.

The criteria for the confirmation of a miracle, as established at the beginning of the century during the so-called scientific period, have not been adapted scientifically and theologically. During that period scientism affirmed categorically that a miracle was absolutely impossible. Faced with this position Christian apologetics sought a quasi-geometric proof for miracles. The theory was: one miracle, absolutely proved, will destroy scientism. But today, scientism, with its naive pretensions, is dead. The equally naive pretension to absolute proof has led miracles to a cul-de-sac. Even though the doctors in charge of the confirmation of cures have introduced the veto clause which up to this set aside the validity of their evidence: 'inexplicable in the present state of science', eleven years have passed without recognition of one miracle at Lourdes (between May 1965 and May 1976). The two exceptions that have appeared since: V. Micheli (254 May 1976) and Serge Perrin (17 June 1978) give the impression of being the end of the line with the sole exception of little Delizia Cirolli, whose dossier, though medically complete, remains in limbo in a Sicilian diocese. We appear to be moving towards the extinction of the confirmation of miracles. It is not that Christ no longer cures. Rather we are no longer capable of welcoming and recognising these cures. For the past fifteen years, I have been discreetly voicing my opinion that we ought to revise this situation as well as the criteria for recognition, in agreement with several observations from Dr Mangiapan which could be used as an outline for such a revision. Two things are desirable:

— In the Church we must know how to accept faith in miraculous cures, which Christ not only highlighted in his ministry, but also recommended to his disciples (*Mt 10, 8; Mt 16, 18; Mt 10, 9*), and we must also learn to give thanks (following the example of the tenth leper). The confirmation ought to verify, channel, sometimes moderate this thanksgiving, but not systematically repress it or impose a gloomy silence.

— Today, those who have been cured by the hand of the Lord are sometimes very surprised at the poor reception they are given by the established medical or religious authorities, when they announce this good news to the Church. This has the appearance of ill-considered haste and imprudence and a type of aggression towards the authorities whose task is the recognition of miracles. It is true that Jesus imposed silence on those he cured, but, they did not observe it and the Gospel does not blame them. When we take into account the particular tactical reasons Christ had for maintaining a degree of silence about his threatened ministry, today's silence does not appear to be necessarŷ. What seems to be more desirable is to find a better connection between hope and the gift of God, between the gift and the confirmation, between the thanksgiving and the official stamp. The sullen attitude with regard to the cures which God continues to effect derives in part from an attention to minutiae which is out of place in the Gospel and reminds us of the attitude of the Scribes and Pharisees in the presence of the man born blind. In so far as the confirmation of a miracle is concerned it should not be pursued in the same way as one would look for absolute or quasi-geometric proof.

Such a method conforms neither with the Gospel nor the tradition of the Church nor the way in which God works. It is a remarkable fact that the Church, which has condemned so much in matters of doctrine and morals, has never issued a condemnation in relation to cures, even though cures have never ceased over the centuries.

It no longer conforms with scientific requirements. Today science thinks in terms of probability. Recognition of cures ought, therefore, to espouse this more adult science which has gone beyond the naive approach of scientism and old-fashioned apologetics.

4. The luminous phenomena of Medjugorje pose a delicate and badly-defined problem which we should approach with prudence. We draw no conclusion about them. However, eliminating these facts by simply avoiding noting them officially (as has been done up to now), or by giving them *a priori* a pejorative label (illusion, hallucination) or a pseudo-scientific label (thermionic or geomagnetic phenomena etc.), is to adopt a sterile procedure.

Are the 'signs in the heaven' of which Christ speaks only the mythology of a dead past? Could they in fact correspond to a reality in those last days for which Christ announced them? Do such signs have unknown material causes or do they have a transcendent cause? These questions remain open. There is no *a priori* reason for closing them and it would be as foolish to put them aside lightly as it would be to explain them hastily.

5. As for the hypothesis which states that Medjugorje would be the work of the devil, we confined our brief examination to an appendix because, in spite of the wide publicity received by this thesis in many languages, it remains artificial. Those who support it have not seen the reality: not the visionaries, the ecstasies, the parish with its spiritual life, nor the growing movement of fasting and towards conversion etc. Those for whom Vatican II was the work of the devil see the conformity of the apparitions of Medjugorje to the Council as a diabolic work. For those who understand Fatima as bellicose anti-communism the invitation for reconciliation through love of one's enemies that issues from Medjugorje is a capitualation to the devil. The brilliant dialectic put at the service of these and other ideological presuppositions does not fool anyone. If the devil was promoting prayer (including the rosary, conversion, confession on a large scale, penance, fasting, reconciliation etc.) we would have to say that he had been converted. Let us be serious.

For many Christians Medjugorje awakened the almost forgotten conviction that God, Christ and the Virgin are real beings who are near us, converse with us and guide our lives at a personal and collective level, and that an encounter with them is capable of transforming and transfiguring us. Ecstasies, cures and other graces from Medjugorje are the remarkable signs of this. Conversations and letters that are overwhelming are for me a daily manifestation of this authentic phenomenon of grace.

Our scientific studies do not elucidate this essential core. They verify its medical impacts: physical and psychic. They show its coherence, but do not explain it. They circumscribe the phenomena but come up against a boundary beyond which our instruments do not go. The visionaries appear as receivers who are centred on a transmitter which they perceive as objective, but which remains outside our grasp. Our scientific studies can neither prove nor exclude its existence but can indicate it as the most coherent explanation of a phenomenon that would otherwise be inexplicable and that could not be reduced to the pathological.

Those who are sensitive to the religious character of the apparitions deplore the indiscretion of those tests which treat the sacred as a guinea-pig. Some of the photographs in this book shock them. Perhaps this was also the first reaction of the visionaries? But the visionaries understood that these verifications, which would be useful for them and for believers, could also be useful for sceptics in good faith. These tests were also a risk, because if there was any question of cheating or if the ecstasy turned out to be a pathological phenomenon, the tests would no doubt have provided evidence of this. It was with this in view that the visionaries agreed to ask the Virgin's permission to allow this test and it is with her consent and theirs that we proceeded with these unprecedented experiments. The tests achieved their end by excluding reductionist eplanations and by confirming the likelihood of the simple and ingenuous explanation given by the visionaries: a gratuitous encounter with she who guides them and gives them an impressive message for a world in danger.

Our scientific study remained modestly within the proper bounds, on the threshold of this twilight zone in which God gives himself as a viaticum for our earthly journey.